Eyewitness
HURRICANE & TORNADO

Cyclone shelter

Spots on the sun

Sunset at Stonehenge, England

19th-century reproduction of Galileo's original thermoscope

Saturn

Lighthouse at the George Washington Bridge in New York, USA

Wind-eroded rocks in Utah, USA

Ice crystal

Pine cone with open scales indicating dry weather

Eyewitness
HURRICANE & TORNADO

Written by
JACK CHALLONER

Simultaneous waterspout and lightning bolt

Doppler-radar dome

Storm system on Earth viewed from space

Avalanche-warning sign

DK

LONDON, NEW YORK,
MELBOURNE, MUNICH, AND DELHI

Project editor Melanie Halton
Art editor Ann Cannings
Managing editor Sue Grabham
Senior managing art editor Julia Harris
Editorial consultant Lesley Newson
Picture research Mollie Gillard, Samantha Nunn
DTP designers Andrew O'Brien, Georgia Bryer
Production Kate Oliver

PAPERBACK EDITION
Managing editor Andrew Macintyre
Managing art editor Jane Thomas
Senior editor Kitty Blount
Editor and reference compiler Sarah Phillips
Art editor Andrew Nash
Production Jenny Jacoby
Picture research Bridget Tilly
DTP Designer Siu Yin Ho
Consultant David Glover

This Eyewitness ® Guide has been conceived by
Dorling Kindersley Limited and Editions Gallimard

Hardback edition first published in Great Britain in 2000
This edition published in Great Britain in 2004
by Dorling Kindersley Limited,
80 Strand, London WC2 0RL

2 4 6 8 10 9 7 5 3 1

Copyright © 2000, © 2004 Dorling Kindersley Limited,
London
Penguin Group

A CIP catalogue record for this book is
available from the British Library.

ISBN 1 4053 0296 8

Colour reproduction by
Colourscan, Singapore
Printed in Singapore by Toppan, China

See our complete
catalogue at

www.dk.com

Storm erupts on the sun

Venetian blind twisted by a tornado

Italian thermometer (1657)

Hurricane-warning flags

Contents

Icicle formation
in Arizona, USA

Weather folklore

I<small>N ANCIENT TIMES</small>, people had very little idea how the weather worked. Some realized that clouds were made of water, but they could not work out where the wind came from, and did not understand the sun. Many believed that the gods made the weather, so weather mythology is often associated with religion. Others relied on guesses based on simple observations of plants, animals, or the sky to make forecasts. Ideas and observations were handed down from generation to generation, as sayings or stories, and some are quite reliable. But only when we understand fully how the weather works can we predict it with any accuracy. Weather science began in ancient Greece, when philosophers tried to explain what caused the weather. Some of their ideas were correct, but they did not test their theories, so they were often wrong.

CONE WATCH
No one knows when people first noticed that pine cones open their scales in dry air and close them when the air is humid. But because the air normally becomes more humid before rainfall, pine cones can be used to forecast wet weather.

PHENOMENAL THINKERS
Philosophers Aristotle and Plato were among the first people to try to explain scientifically how the weather works. They lived about 2,400 years ago in ancient Greece, and wrote about cloud, hail, storm, and snow formation, and more unusual phenomena, such as sun haloes. Their ideas were very influential and were not challenged until about 2,000 years later.

Detail from an Italian fresco showing Plato and Aristotle (1511)

CRY FOR RAIN
These Yali tribesmen of New Guinea are performing a dance to call for rain. Without rain there will be no harvest. During part of this ritual, dancers carry grass, which is believed to pierce the eye of the sun, making it cry tears of rain.

ANIMAL FORECASTS
Many animals respond to changes in temperature, humidity, or atmospheric pressure. Cocks, for example, often crow, and mistlethrushes sing, just before a thunderstorm. Observing animal behaviour can therefore be a useful way of making weather forecasts.

SUN WORSHIP

Since the beginning of recorded history, many cultures have worshipped the sun. Stonehenge, in England, is one of many ancient sites thought to have been a place of sun worship. Some of the stones line up to the point where the sun rises on the summer solstice (the day the sun is at its highest in the sky).

Stonehenge was built between about 3000 BC and 1500 BC

WATCHING THE SKY

An ancient Maori myth describes how the god of thunder and lightning, Tawhaki, went up to the sky disguised as a kite. Maori priests believed they could predict the weather by watching how kites, which they flew in Tawhaki's honour, moved across the sky.

Maori kite made of canvas and twigs

MAGIC CHARMS

This figurehead from the Solomon Islands would have been attached to the front of a canoe to ward off dangerous storms at sea. Many lucky charms, used by people to protect themselves against bad weather, are linked to gods or spirits. The charms may be hung from ceilings, placed in fireplaces, or worn as jewellery.

Statue of Mayan rain god, Chac, used for worship

STORMY TALE

In the Shinto religion that originated in Japan, Amaterasu Omikami is the "divine being who lights up heaven". Her brother is a storm god, and when he causes strong winds and floods, Amaterasu is so disappointed that she hides in a cave. This makes the world go dark, just as it seems to do during a storm.

Bushy-tailed squirrel

WEATHER SACRIFICE

According to legend, the Mayan rain god, Chac, sent rain for the crops. But he also sent storms, which destroyed crops and flooded villages. People hoped that if they made offerings to Chac, the rains would continue to fall, but the storms would cease.

FURRY TALE

Some people believe that the bushier a squirrel's tail during autumn, the harsher the winter will be. There is no scientific evidence that this idea is correct.

Early forecasts

Glass bulb

THE MODERN SCIENCE of the weather is called meteorology. This science would not have been possible without discovering the behaviour of the components – water, heat, and air – that make the weather. It was about 300 years ago that people first began to experiment scientifically with these elements. Through their experiments, they learnt about atmospheric pressure, which gases make up the air, and why water disappears as it evaporates. Early meteorologists invented a variety of crude measuring instruments that allowed them to test their theories, and devise new ones. Two of the most important developments were the thermometer for measuring temperatures, and the barometer, which measures atmospheric pressure. Another vital device is the hygrometer, which measures humidity – the concentration of water in the air. Nowadays, using sophisticated equipment, meteorologists can predict the arrival of extreme weather conditions, such as hurricanes, with great accuracy.

UNDER PRESSURE
In 1643, Italian physicist Evangelista Torricelli (1608–47) made the first barometer. He filled a 1-m (3-ft) long, glass tube with mercury, and placed it upside down in a bowl of mercury. The mercury column dropped to about 76 cm (30 in). Torricelli realized that it was the weight, or pressure, of air on the mercury in the bowl that stopped the mercury in the tube from falling further.

MOVING MERCURY
The inventor of this mercury barometer was meteorologist Robert Fitzroy. His barometer has a scale in inches to measure the height of the mercury column. Fine weather is forecast when atmospheric pressure pushes the mercury column above 76 cm (30 in). Unsettled weather is likely when the mercury falls below this measurement.

Fitzroy barometer

HIGH TEMPERATURE
Italian physicist Galileo Galilei (1564–1642) designed this thermoscope, an early thermometer, about 400 years ago. It indicated changes in temperature but was unable to give exact readings. A long tube with a bulb at the end sat in a flask of water. Air in the bulb expanded as the temperature rose causing the water level in the tube to drop. The air contracted as it became cooler, raising the water level.

INVISIBLE WATER
Air normally becomes very humid before a thunderstorm. The water in the air is an invisible vapour. You may not be able to see it, but you can measure it. This hygrometer, designed about 350 years ago, does just that. Water is absorbed from the air by the cotton bag, which becomes slightly heavier. The greater the humidity, the more the bag drops down.

Flask would have been filled with water

Cotton bag for absorbing moisture in the air

Balancing weight made of glass

A 19th-century reproduction of Galileo's original thermoscope

17th-century balance hygrometer

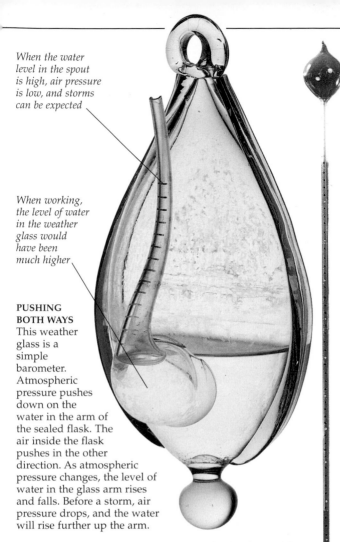

When the water level in the spout is high, air pressure is low, and storms can be expected

When working, the level of water in the weather glass would have been much higher

PUSHING BOTH WAYS
This weather glass is a simple barometer. Atmospheric pressure pushes down on the water in the arm of the sealed flask. The air inside the flask pushes in the other direction. As atmospheric pressure changes, the level of water in the glass arm rises and falls. Before a storm, air pressure drops, and the water will rise further up the arm.

A QUESTION OF SCALE
When this thermometer was made, in 1657, there was no agreed scale for reading measurements. If you want to use a thermometer to take accurate temperatures, rather than just "hot" or "cold", your thermometer needs a scale. Today, meteorologists use two main scales to record temperature – Celsius and Fahrenheit. Both of these scales were invented in the 18th century.

Ornate thermometer made in Italy, 1657

HOTTING UP
The long, spiralling tube of this glass thermometer is designed to save space. When the temperature increases, water in the lower bulb expands, filling more space in the spiral tube. The higher the water level in the tube, the higher the temperature.

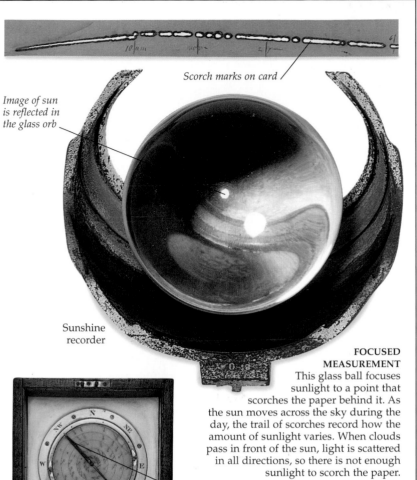

Scorch marks on card

Image of sun is reflected in the glass orb

Sunshine recorder

FOCUSED MEASUREMENT
This glass ball focuses sunlight to a point that scorches the paper behind it. As the sun moves across the sky during the day, the trail of scorches record how the amount of sunlight varies. When clouds pass in front of the sun, light is scattered in all directions, so there is not enough sunlight to scorch the paper.

Thick needle aligns with the normal path of storms in the region

Thin needle indicates safe course away from the storm

KEEPING AN EYE ON THE STORM
Before radio warnings, sailors used this clever device, called a barocyclonometer, to calculate the position of approaching hurricanes. Cyclonic winds spiral at their centre, where the atmospheric pressure is very low. By measuring how atmospheric pressure and wind direction change, sailors could work out the general direction in which a hurricane was moving and steer their vessels to safety.

IT'S A GAS
During the 1770s, French chemist Antoine Lavoisier (1743–94) made important discoveries about the atmosphere. He was the first person to discover that the atmosphere is a mixture of gases. He also found that hydrogen and oxygen combine to make water.

What is extreme weather?

Hurricanes, tornadoes, droughts, floods, or freezing temperatures – extreme weather – can endanger people's lives or damage their crops or property. The weather at any time can be described by temperature, wind speed, atmospheric pressure, and precipitation (rain, hail, or snow). The average temperature of the world is about 15°C (59°F), but some places are much colder than this, other places much warmer. The average rainfall across the world is 100 cm (39 in) per year. But the rain is not evenly distributed – some parts of the world have virtually no rain at all, others as much as 11 m (36 ft) in one year. Also, a particular location may be dry for months and then be soaked by a flood. Often, extreme weather takes people by surprise. Destructive thunderstorms, tornadoes, or floods can happen in places where weather is normally quite calm.

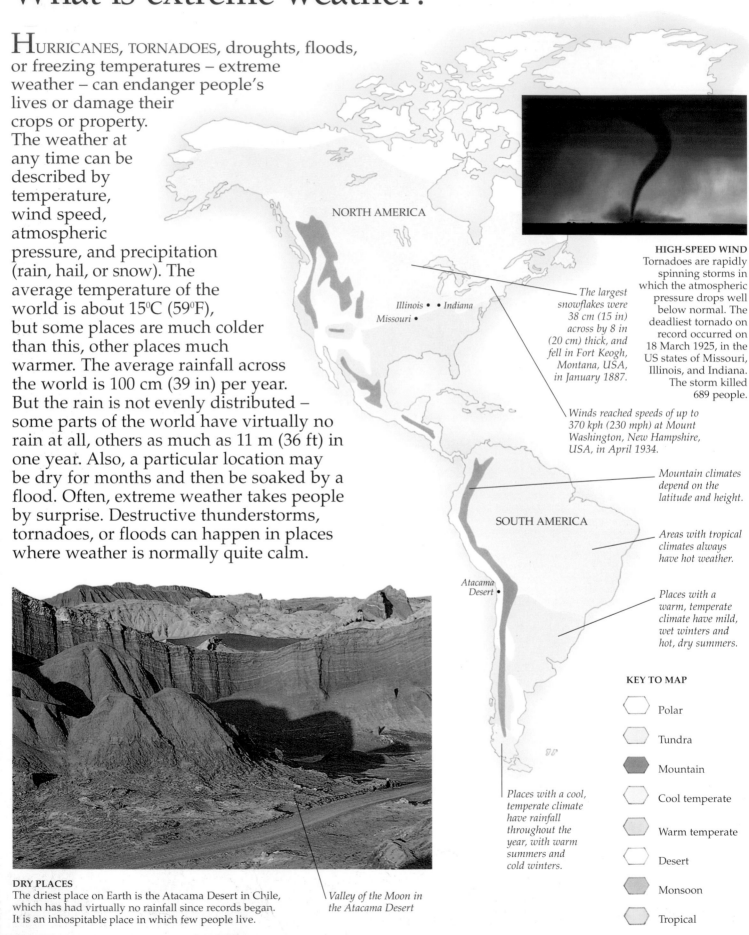

NORTH AMERICA

Illinois • • Indiana
Missouri •

The largest snowflakes were 38 cm (15 in) across by 8 in (20 cm) thick, and fell in Fort Keogh, Montana, USA, in January 1887.

Winds reached speeds of up to 370 kph (230 mph) at Mount Washington, New Hampshire, USA, in April 1934.

HIGH-SPEED WIND
Tornadoes are rapidly spinning storms in which the atmospheric pressure drops well below normal. The deadliest tornado on record occurred on 18 March 1925, in the US states of Missouri, Illinois, and Indiana. The storm killed 689 people.

Mountain climates depend on the latitude and height.

SOUTH AMERICA

Areas with tropical climates always have hot weather.

Atacama
Desert •

Places with a warm, temperate climate have mild, wet winters and hot, dry summers.

KEY TO MAP

⬡ Polar

⬡ Tundra

⬡ Mountain

⬡ Cool temperate

⬡ Warm temperate

⬡ Desert

⬡ Monsoon

⬡ Tropical

Places with a cool, temperate climate have rainfall throughout the year, with warm summers and cold winters.

DRY PLACES
The driest place on Earth is the Atacama Desert in Chile, which has had virtually no rainfall since records began. It is an inhospitable place in which few people live.

Valley of the Moon in the Atacama Desert

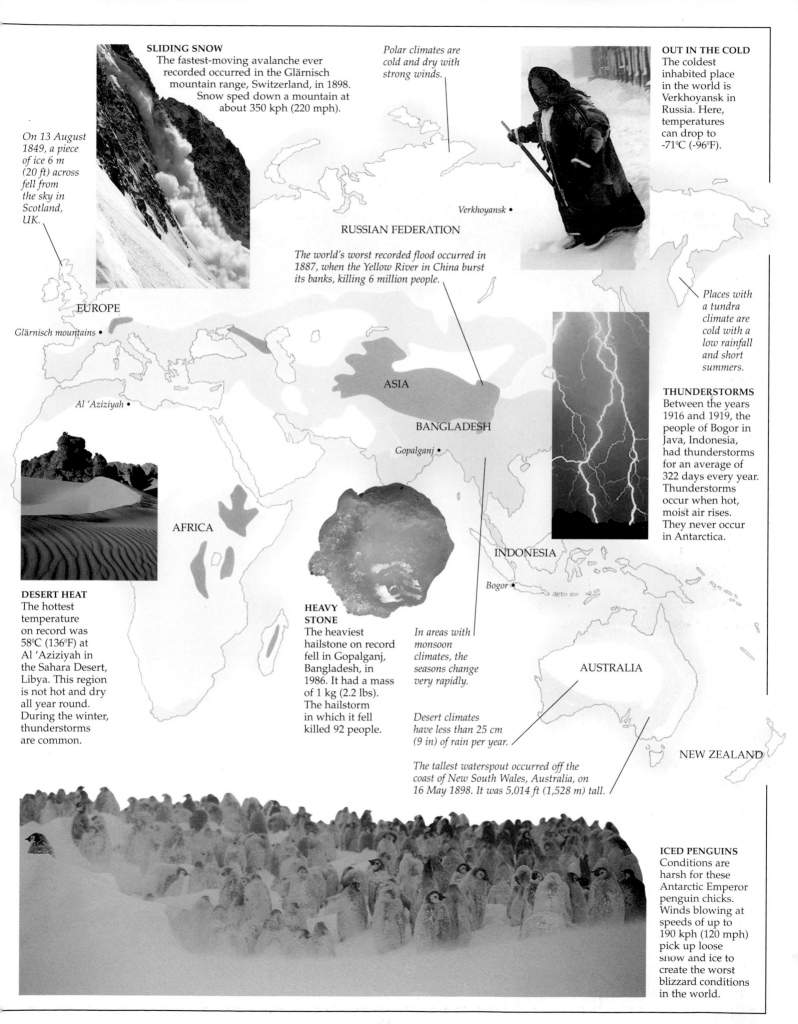

SLIDING SNOW
The fastest-moving avalanche ever recorded occurred in the Glärnisch mountain range, Switzerland, in 1898. Snow sped down a mountain at about 350 kph (220 mph).

Polar climates are cold and dry with strong winds.

OUT IN THE COLD
The coldest inhabited place in the world is Verkhoyansk in Russia. Here, temperatures can drop to -71⁰C (-96⁰F).

On 13 August 1849, a piece of ice 6 m (20 ft) across fell from the sky in Scotland, UK.

Verkhoyansk •

RUSSIAN FEDERATION

The world's worst recorded flood occurred in 1887, when the Yellow River in China burst its banks, killing 6 million people.

EUROPE

Glärnisch mountains •

Places with a tundra climate are cold with a low rainfall and short summers.

ASIA

Al 'Aziziyah •

BANGLADESH

Gopalganj •

THUNDERSTORMS
Between the years 1916 and 1919, the people of Bogor in Java, Indonesia, had thunderstorms for an average of 322 days every year. Thunderstorms occur when hot, moist air rises. They never occur in Antarctica.

AFRICA

INDONESIA

Bogor •

DESERT HEAT
The hottest temperature on record was 58⁰C (136⁰F) at Al 'Aziziyah in the Sahara Desert, Libya. This region is not hot and dry all year round. During the winter, thunderstorms are common.

HEAVY STONE
The heaviest hailstone on record fell in Gopalganj, Bangladesh, in 1986. It had a mass of 1 kg (2.2 lbs). The hailstorm in which it fell killed 92 people.

In areas with monsoon climates, the seasons change very rapidly.

Desert climates have less than 25 cm (9 in) of rain per year.

AUSTRALIA

The tallest waterspout occurred off the coast of New South Wales, Australia, on 16 May 1898. It was 5,014 ft (1,528 m) tall.

NEW ZEALAND

ICED PENGUINS
Conditions are harsh for these Antarctic Emperor penguin chicks. Winds blowing at speeds of up to 190 kph (120 mph) pick up loose snow and ice to create the worst blizzard conditions in the world.

Causes of extreme weather

THERE ARE MANY FACTORS that can affect the weather. Among the most important are the heating of the Earth by the sun and differences in atmospheric pressure. Low atmospheric pressure usually means stormy weather. The pressure at the centre of a hurricane is extremely low, for example. Other factors, including dust from volcanoes or storms on the sun's surface, can disturb the weather, making it hotter or colder, or increasing or reducing rainfall. Humans can also affect the weather by polluting the atmosphere. Although the causes of extreme weather are well understood, it is still impossible to predict weather more than a few days ahead. This is because the weather is a very complex system that is very sensitive to small disturbances. It has been said that even the beat of a butterfly's wing could affect how the weather develops.

CHAOTIC WEATHER
While a butterfly cannot be said to cause floods and storms, it can, in theory, change the course of the weather. This is the strange conclusion of chaos theory – the study of unpredictable systems such as the weather. It is believed that the weather is so sensitive to atmospheric conditions that the slightest change in air movement, such as that caused by a tiny flapping wing, can alter the course of the world's weather.

SPOTTING BAD WEATHER
Dark, cool patches with a diameter of several thousand kilometres sometimes appear on the surface of the sun, and last for about a week. These sunspots throw out debris that can reach as far as Earth. When this happens, global temperatures can rise, and storms are more frequent. The spots are most numerous every 11 years, and extreme weather on Earth seems to coincide with this cycle.

GLOBAL WARMING
Many of the gases and smoke particles that modern industry and vehicles produce hang in the air. This can bring dramatic and beautiful sunsets, but can also affect the weather. Carbon dioxide released by burning fossil fuels seems to be causing an increase in the world's average temperature. If this "global warming'" continues, it could upset balances in the world's weather. There could be more storms, and the ice-caps may melt, raising sea levels.

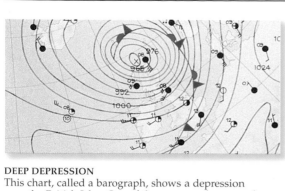

DEEP DEPRESSION

This chart, called a barograph, shows a depression over the British Isles. One of the common features of unsettled weather is a region of air with low atmospheric pressure. This is called a depression, because a lowering of air pressure reduces, or "depresses", the reading on a barometer. A depression forms when air is warmed, expands, and rises. Winds spiral in towards the centre of the depression. The deeper the depression, the stronger the winds.

GREENHOUSE GASES

Chemical compounds called chlorofluorocarbons (CFCs) are released by various industrial processes, and used to be emitted by aerosol cans. CFCs break down an atmospheric gas called ozone, which protects the Earth from harmful ultraviolet radiation. Like carbon dioxide, CFCs are known as "greenhouse gases" because they seem to slowly increase the world's temperature. During the 1990s, most of the world's nations agreed to stop producing CFCs, and aerosol sprays were banned.

HOT AND COLD

The sun is the source of most of the Earth's energy, but some parts of the world receive more energy than others. At the poles, sunlight always hits the Earth's surface at an angle, because of the curvature of the globe. The sun therefore heats the equator more intensely than it does the poles. These temperature differences alter atmospheric pressure. This causes global winds that influence weather patterns.

Sunlight warms the Earth

Sunlight is concentrated at the equator

Sunlight spreads over a greater area at the north and south poles

Equator

GLOBAL COOLING

Mount St Helens (right) in Washington, USA, erupted in 1980. For a few months after the event, climatologists measured a drop of almost 0.5°C (33°F) in the average global temperature. This was due to volcanic dust travelling around the world and blocking out some of the sun's heat and light.

Severe winds

STRONG WINDS CAN WREAK HAVOC. Their force depends on the speed at which they travel. The fastest winds at ground or sea level are found in hurricanes and tornadoes, and both can cause widespread devastation. Higher in the atmosphere are winds that are faster still – jet streams. They are too high up to cause any damage, and are very important because they help to distribute the sun's heat around the world. Global winds are caused by the sun heating various parts of the Earth differently. Local winds, on the other hand, are smaller-scale, and are caused by regional changes in temperature and pressure. To predict wind behaviour, accurate speed measurements are vital.

ALL AT SEA
Francis Beaufort (1774–1857) was a commander in the British Navy. In 1805 he devised a system – the Beaufort Scale – for estimating wind speeds at sea. The system assigns names and numbers to 12 different strengths of wind, from "light air" to "hurricane force". It is still in use today, but modern devices are more accurate.

STANDING TALL
This model shows the design for the 840-m (2,700-ft) tall Millennium Tower proposed for Tokyo, Japan. One of the most important considerations in the design of any skyscraper is wind resistance. Millennium Tower is encircled by a steel frame, which strengthens the building and provides protection from fierce winds.

Architectural model of Millennium Tower, Tokyo

Head faces in the direction from which the wind is blowing

WEATHER VANE
Weather vanes are perhaps the oldest of all meteorological instruments. This weather cock's tail has a larger surface area than its head. The tail swings around as the wind changes direction, and points the cock's head towards the wind. A reading is taken from the direction in which the wind blows. For example, a westerly wind is one that comes from the west and blows to the east.

FLYING IN THE WIND
In March 1999, balloonists Bertrand Piccard and Brian Jones became the first people ever to fly a hot-air balloon nonstop around the world. Their balloon, *Breitling Orbiter 3*, was sometimes assisted by jet-stream winds blowing at up to 300 kph (185 mph). Jet streams can reduce aeroplane flight times from the United States to Europe by up to two hours.

WIND SWEPT
A combination of wind and sand erosion has carved a beautiful landscape into these sandstone rocks. If severe winds blow across the rocks, sweeping up the surface layer of sand, dense and dangerous sandstorms may occur.

Wind vane to show direction

Cups spin around – their speed depends on the strength of the wind

Rotors turn wind vane into the wind

Average wind speed is recorded on graph paper as the cylinder rotates

A man struggles across Chicago's Wabash Avenue Bridge in fierce winds

WIND RECORDER
This clever measuring device was made long before electronic computers existed. It is called an anemometer and records wind speed and direction over a long period of time. In order to understand how the wind works, forecasters need to take as many measurements as possible.

Weathered sandstone, Colorado Plateau, Utah, USA

THE WINDY CITY
During winter, the US city of Chicago is regularly battered by strong winds. Chicago lies near the Great Lakes, where inland air mixes with air from the lakes. Because the atmospheric pressure of these air masses is different, they send gusts of wind around the city as they collide.

SWING BRIDGE
Tacoma Narrows Bridge in Washington, USA, was badly damaged by wind in 1940. Strong gusts caused the bridge to swing – first gently, and then ever more violently. Eventually, the bridge collapsed. Since the winds were not as strong as in a hurricane, the bridge's design was blamed for the disaster.

Thunderous storms

TREMENDOUS AMOUNTS OF ENERGY are released in the torrential rain, strong winds, thunder, and lightning that accompany thunderstorms. The most energetic storms may create hail or even tornadoes. The source of all this energy is the sun, which evaporates water from land or sea. The resulting warm, moist air rises and begins to cool as it does so. Vapour in the cooling air condenses, forming countless tiny water drops and ice crystals that make up a darkening cumulonimbus cloud, or thunderhead. The rising current of air is known as an updraught, and may reach speeds of more than 100 kph (60 mph). When rain or hail falls, it brings with it a downdraught of cooler air. The downdraught spreads out in all directions when it reaches the ground, causing the gusty winds of a thunderstorm.

LETTING GO
Tornadoes, lightning, and inland waterspouts often occur during severe storms as thunderclouds quickly release energy. The large lightning bolt and waterspout seen here occurred during a thunderstorm over Florida, USA.

VIEW FROM THE AIR
This photograph was taken from a spacecraft orbiting around Earth. It shows how a whole system of storms can develop when warm, moist air meets cold, dry air. The cold air undercuts the warm air, lifting it to form pockets of rising air. These pockets show up as thunderheads through the existing blanket of cloud.

WATER CARRIER
A thunderhead is an impressive tower of cloud. The top of the cloud may reach a height of some 12 km (7.5 miles), while its base may loom just 1,000 m (3,280 ft) above ground. A typical thunderhead contains about 10,000 tonnes of water.

THUNDER BEATS
In the Japanese Shinto religion, many forces of nature are worshipped as gods, known as *kami*. Sometimes *kami* are represented as human figures. This Japanese god of thunder is shown as a strong man beating his drum.

Balls of thunder

Thunder shown as a demon in the air

Drumstick to beat out the sound of thunder

Japanese thunder god

- Ice particles
- Snowflakes
- Water drops

Hot, moist air rises

Heavy rain and maybe hail

Cloud begins to run out of energy

LIFE OF A THUNDERSTORM
This diagram explains how a thunderstorm develops. First, an updraught (red arrows) of warm, moist air begins to form the cloud as the moisture evaporates from the air. Water vapour then releases large amounts of heat as it condenses. This heat warms the air further and causes the air to rise higher. The storm finally subsides when the air begins to cool and the downdraught (green arrows) helps to disperse the cloud.

CALM BEFORE THE STORM
Thunderstorms often occur at the end of a hot summer day, when air that has been warmed by the hot ground rises quickly into the cooling air. A thundercloud carries many tonnes of water. These clouds are so dense that they absorb almost all of the light that falls on them. This is why they appear black. Beyond the thunderclouds, the air is clear and calm.

Cloud stops rising and spreads out as it hits a cold dry layer of atmospheric air

SUPERCELL
Most thunderstorms begin as one or more cells (pockets) of rising air. The term "supercell" is used to describe a particularly large and energetic cell, in which air rises more quickly than normal. This type of cell carries a huge amount of water up into the thundercloud. Tornadoes and waterspouts are born from such cells.

Supercell storm cloud in Texas, USA

Strong updraughts carry wisps of cloud high into the atmosphere

Mixture of ice crystals and water

Air is drawn in at the base of the cloud

Twisting tornadoes

TORNADOES HAVE MANY NAMES including whirlwinds and twisters. These high-speed spiralling winds roar past in just a few minutes, but leave behind them a trail of destruction. Meteorologists are not yet certain precisely how tornadoes are formed. They seem to develop at the base of thunderclouds during storms, as warm, moist air rises from the ground and passes through a mass of colder air at the bottom of the cloud. Somehow this draws winds that are already circulating around the storm into a high-speed whirl. The pressure at the centre of a tornado is much lower than that outside. This creates a funnel, or vortex, which acts like a giant vacuum cleaner, sucking up anything in its path.

A tornado funnel appears at the base of a thundercloud

1 WALL OF CLOUD
This series of photographs clearly shows how a tornado develops. The funnel of the tornado descends from a thundercloud above. A column of cloud then forms as moisture as the air condenses in the low pressure inside the tornado.

Swirling black thundercloud indicates the start of a tornado

Funnel changes colour as it picks up debris

2 DOWN TO EARTH
This tornado is passing over dusty farmland. So, when the base of the tornado meets the ground, the funnel becomes partly obscured by dust picked up by the rising air and swirling winds.

LIQUID FUNNEL
When a tornado passes over a lake or the sea, the updraught at its centre sucks up water, forming a waterspout. The wind speeds inside a waterspout are much less than in ordinary tornadoes – as low as 80 kph (50 mph) – partly due to the weight of the water they carry.

Funnel narrows as the tornado's energy diminishes

3 LOSING POWER
Energy from the tornado's winds throws debris into the air. As the tornado loses energy, it slows down. Eventually, the funnel will shrink back to the thundercloud from which it was born.

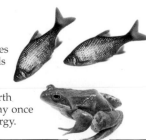

STRANGE DOWNPOURS
When a tornado passes over water, small animals such as frogs and fish may be lifted high into the air, only to fall to Earth again some distance away once the tornado loses its energy.

SPIN CYCLE
A tornado is a writhing funnel of rapidly spinning air that descends to the ground from the base of a large thundercloud. At the heart of a tornado is a low-pressure vortex, which acts like a huge vacuum cleaner, sucking up air and anything the tornado encounters on the ground.

KICKING UP DUST
Dust devils, like waterspouts, are whirlwinds, which are common in desert regions. Although less energetic and less destructive than tornadoes, they are created in the same way. Air above the hot desert sand begins to rise quickly, producing the updraught necessary for the whirlwind to form. The circling winds typically reach speeds of about 40 kph (25 mph).

Tornado force

THE VIOLENT SWIRLING WINDS of a tornado are among the most destructive forces in nature. With speeds of up to 500 kph (310 mph), these winds can tear houses apart, wrap cars around trees, and kill or injure any living thing in their path. A violent tornado can devastate a whole community, destroying all the buildings in its path. Most of the world's destructive tornadoes occur during the summer in the mid-western states of the USA, where cold air from Canada in the north sits on top of warm, moist air from the Gulf of Mexico to the south. This region is often referred to as Tornado Alley. Meteorologists still cannot fully explain the mechanisms that cause tornadoes, and predicting where and when they will occur proves even more difficult.

TOWERING TORNADO
The destructive vortex (spinning centre) of a tornado is usually about 2 km (1 mile) wide. Dust or objects at ground level are lifted high into the air and are flung sideways or kept in the air to be deposited later when the tornado winds down. Tornadoes typically sweep over the land at speeds of about 55 kph (35 mph), leaving behind them a trail of devastation.

Venetian blind twisted by a tornado

Tornado funnel descends from a thundercloud

BLIND PANIC
The air pressure inside a tornado is much lower than normal. When a tornado passed by this window, the window exploded outwards, because air pressure inside the room was higher than outside. Much of the destruction of a tornado is caused by the sudden drop in pressure that it brings.

This door was sucked out of the window by the tornado's force

TORNADO ALLEY
This map highlights an area in the United States known as Tornado Alley, which includes parts of the states of Kansas, Oklahoma, and Missouri. This region experiences several hundred tornadoes every year. Tornadoes claim about 100 lives each year in the United States.

CANADA

UNITED STATES

Kansas • • Missouri
• Oklahoma

MEXICO

Areas most at risk from tornadoes

BLOWN AWAY
The worshippers in this church in Piedmont, Virginia, USA, were caught by surprise when a tornado struck during a service, in March 1994. The force of the tornado ripped the roof off the church.

Dust and debris is swept up as the tornado passes over the ground

IN A TWIST
The incredible power of a tornado is shown in this photograph of what was once a truck. Winds travelling at more than 400 kph (250 mph) picked up the truck and hurled it down again, leaving behind a mess of twisted steel.

Twisting column of cloud

Swirling vortex

A tornado rips a house apart in the 1998 film Twister

STORM CHASING
In the United States some people deliberately pursue tornadoes in order to learn more about them. These storm chasers, in their specially equipped trucks, are called into action when a "tornado watch" warning is issued by the National Weather Service.

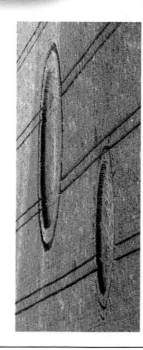

CIRCLES OF MYSTERY
For centuries, strange and unexplained circles of flattened crops have appeared in fields across the world. Some people believe that tornadoes are responsible for many of these circles. But this is unlikely since tornadoes do not tend to hover over one spot for long enough – instead, they move across the land, leaving a trail of destruction.

STRANGE TALES
Tornadoes often leave behind bizarre stories. A chicken in Alabama, USA, is reported to have survived tornadic winds of about 200 kph (120 mph), which stripped it of its tail and feathers.

Lightning strikes

NEARLY TWO THOUSAND thunderstorms occur at any one time across the world. The most impressive feature of a thunderstorm is lightning. Flashes and bolts of lightning are caused by an electric charge that builds up inside a thundercloud. Air inside the cloud rises at speeds of up to 100 kph (60 mph). Tiny ice crystals are carried to the top of the cloud by the moving air, rubbing against pellets of hail as they do so. The ice crystals become positively charged while the hail becomes negatively charged. A lightning bolt is the way in which the electric charges are neutralized – simply huge sparks between cloud and ground, or between the top and bottom of a cloud. The most common form of lightning is fork lightning, but there are other, less common forms, such as ribbon lightning.

STORMY GOD
Before scientists began to explain weather patterns, many cultures believed that the weather was controlled by gods. The Norse god of thunder, Thor, was believed to have made thunderbolts with his magic hammer.

Fossilized lightning bolt

SAND SCULPTURE
This strange shape is made of sand that has melted and then solidified in the path of a lightning strike. The resulting mineral is called fulgurite. The temperature inside a bolt of lightning reaches 30,000°C (54,000°F) – about five times the temperature of the surface of the sun.

BRIGHT SPARK
During a thunderstorm, in 1752, American politician and scientist Benjamin Franklin carried out a dangerous experiment. He flew a kite, with metal objects attached to its string, high into the sky. The metal items produced sparks, proving that electricity had passed along the wet string.

PERSONAL SAFETY
An interesting fashion accessory of the 18th century was the Franklin wire. Invented by Benjamin Franklin in 1753, the metallic wire was suspended from an umbrella or hat and dragged along the ground to divert lightning strikes away from the wearer.

Lightning conductors were all the rage in Paris, 1778

LIGHTNING RODS
Tall buildings, such as the Eiffel Tower (above) in Paris, France, are regular targets for lightning strikes. Metal rods called lightning conductors protect buildings to which they are attached by conducting the electricity safely to the ground.

This tree has been torn apart by lightning

QUICK AS A FLASH
Time-lapse photography captured the many successive lightning flashes of this storm in the USA. A lightning strike begins as a barely visible "leader stroke" at the base of a thundercloud. The leader stroke forms a path of charged atoms, along which huge quantities of electric charge pass incredibly quickly, producing a bright glow. The temperature of the air along this path heats up rapidly and expands, creating a shock wave that is heard as a loud thunderclap.

FORCE OF LIGHTNING
The power of lightning can virtually demolish a building or kill outright a person or animal unfortunate enough to be struck. Trees are particularly vulnerable to lightning strikes because the moist layer below the bark acts as a conductor.

Cloud illuminated from within by a lightning bolt

SKY LIGHTS
Most bolts of lightning do not strike at ground level – they occur within a cloud. A powerful electric current passes between the positively charged top of the cloud, and its negatively charged base. Sometimes, lightning can pass between two neighbouring clouds.

Hailstorms

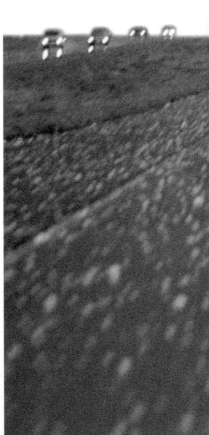

Combating hail in cotton fields in the Fergana Valley, Russia

BALLS OF ICE CALLED HAILSTONES are produced during thunderstorms. The strong vertical air currents in a thundercloud force lumps of ice up and down inside the cloud. With each upward movement the hailstones collect another layer of ice. They continue to grow in size until they are too big to be lifted again by the up-currents. The stronger the up-current, the heavier a hailstone can become. Individual stones with a mass of more than 700 g (1.6 lbs) have been recorded. Stones of this weight require an updraught of more than 150 kph (95 mph). Hailstones that heavy can be life-threatening, but any hailstorm can cause serious damage. Among the worst storms in recent history was one that occurred in Munich, Germany, in July 1984. Financial losses were estimated to have totalled £625 million ($1 billion).

CLOUD BURSTING
People in many parts of the world have searched for ways to save their crops from hail damage. The Russians have, perhaps, had the most success. By firing chemical substances into thunderclouds they have been able to make potential hail fall as harmless rain. This technique has saved vast prairies of grain that could otherwise have been flattened by hail within minutes.

HEAVY STORM
Hailstones are usually about the size of a pea. They bounce when they hit a hard surface, and tend to settle, forming a strange ice-white carpet. Stones do, however, vary in size, and storms vary in severity. In the USA alone, a single hailstorm can cause property damage in excess of £300 million ($500 million), and crop damage amounting to about £185 million ($300 million).

Maize crop destroyed by a severe hailstorm

HAIL ALLEY
Vast regions of the US are under the constant threat of hailstorms. One area in particular, a belt of land spanning from Texas to Montana, known as "Hail Alley", regularly experiences severe hailstorms. Farmers in this region need to spend huge amounts on hail insurance. Yet, little has been done in the US to explore methods of crop protection.

Vehicles pelted by hail during a storm in Texas, USA, in May 1977

DANGEROUS DRIVING
Driving through a hailstorm is extremely hazardous because vehicles skid easily on the hard, icy stones. The severity of damage caused by falling hail depends on the wind speed during a storm. Hailstones with a diameter of 10 cm (4 in), such as the one that hit this windscreen, travel at speeds of up to 170 kph (106 mph).

Windscreen shattered by a hailstone during a storm near Burlington, Colorado, USA, in 1990

This hailstone is the size of a grapefruit

ICE PACK
Hailstones are made up of layers – a bit like onions. Each layer represents one journey through the cloud in which the stone formed. This hailstone – one of the largest ever found – had a diameter of about 19 cm (7.5 in), and a mass of 766 g (1.67 lbs). It has been cut in half and photographed through polarizing filters to show the layers inside the stone.

Cross-section of a hailstone

BIG CHILL
Large hailstones normally fall from "supercell" thunderclouds, which typically have one very strong updraught. This 10-cm (4-in) diameter hailstone fell near Breckenridge in Colorado, USA, in May 1978.

Drivers park their vehicles at the side of the road as they wait for the danger to pass

27

Hurricane alert

THE WORD "HURRICANE" has many origins, including the Native American Taino word "hurucane", meaning "evil spirit of the wind". Hurricanes are officially called "tropical cyclones", but also have several other names, including cyclones in the Indian Ocean, and typhoons in the Pacific. They are huge, rotating storms, which can bring widespread devastation, with winds of up to 350 kph (210 mph), heavy rain, and stormy seas. A hurricane begins as a region of heated air over the warm seas in the tropics – parts of the world near the equator. The heated air expands and rises, creating an area of low pressure air. The surrounding air moves in towards the lower pressure, and is made to spin by the Earth's rotation. Predicting hurricanes is not easy, but weather satellites enable forecasters to give a few days' advance warning.

WINDY WARNING
The destruction caused by a hurricane can be reduced, and lives saved, if a warning is given. These flags are one way to alert people to hurricane danger.

Many buildings were wrecked when a cyclone hit Albany, Georgia, USA (1940)

GALE FORCE
The destructive force of a hurricane comes largely from its strong winds, which spiral in towards the centre of the storm. As more and more air is drawn in towards the centre of the storm, wind speeds increase – just as ice-skaters can spin faster by tucking in their arms.

19th-century aneroid barometer

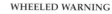

UNDER PRESSURE
A barometer shows the push of the air, caused by the weight of the atmosphere – this push is called atmospheric pressure. The pressure is very low in a hurricane, and changes in pressure can help forecasters to predict approaching storms.

WHEELED WARNING
In areas where few people have radios or televisions, warnings may be delivered in other ways. This man is cycling around a village in Bangladesh, using a megaphone to shout out a hurricane warning.

WATER, WATER EVERYWHERE
Under the low pressure air at the centre of the storm, the sea level bulges to as much as 3 m (12 ft) higher than normal. This swell of water can submerge large areas of coastline, and is responsible for most of the deaths caused by hurricanes.

A community in Bangladesh waits for the threat of a hurricane to pass

Stilts raise this purpose-built cyclone shelter above the ground

SAFETY ON STILTS
Floods are very common during a hurricane – from heavy rains and, in coastal areas, high waves from stormy seas. This shelter is raised above the ground so that flood waters can pass beneath it without endangering lives. The building is specially designed to withstand high winds.

SPINNING CYCLONES
Hurricanes are a type of tropical cyclone. A cyclone is an area of low-pressure air with winds that spiral inwards – clockwise in the southern hemisphere and anti-clockwise in the northern hemisphere. Hurricanes initially move west from their origin near the equator, but many curve back towards the east as they cross the tropic lines.

Northern hemisphere

Equator

NEW GUINEA

AUSTRALIA

Southern hemisphere

VIEW FROM ABOVE
Hurricanes form where the temperature of the sea is above 27°C (80°F). A low pressure, or depression, forms and, once wind speeds reach 62 kph (39 mph), it is classified as a tropical storm. When winds reach 118 kph (74 mph), the storm becomes a hurricane. A hurricane picks up about two billion tonnes of water, as vapour, from the ocean each day. This vapour condenses to form clouds, such as those shown right. One bizarre feature of a hurricane is its eye, or centre. Conditions in the eye are very calm, while all around it are thick clouds and high-speed winds.

The eye of a storm can be up to 50 km (32 miles) wide

Satellite view of Hurricane Emilia (1994)

Hurricane horror

SOME REGIONS OF THE WORLD are more prone to hurricane devastation than others. Areas outside the tropics – more than 2,500 km (1,500 miles) from the equator – are much less at risk than tropical regions. This is because the seas are cooler far from the equator, providing less energy to fuel hurricanes. The northeast coast of South America is an area often hit because it lies in the path of hurricanes that form just north of the equator, and move northwest in the Atlantic Ocean. Hurricanes bring huge waves, known as storm surges, which cause the biggest loss of lives. But it is the strong winds that cause the greatest destruction – they have no regard for people's homes or possessions.

The hurricane of 1900 demolished this school in Galveston, but the desks are still screwed tightly to the floor

AMERICAN TRAGEDY
One of the deadliest hurricanes experienced in the US struck the coastal city of Galveston, Texas, in September 1900. More than 12,000 people died, 2,600 homes were destroyed, and about 10,000 people were left homeless. A protective wall was constructed around the rebuilt city, and has successfully protected it from hurricane tidal waves ever since.

Hurricane David's powerful winds have lifted this plane into the air, and deposited it on top of a hangar

ROOFTOP LANDING
The Dominican Republic was struck by a particularly dangerous and destructive hurricane in August 1979. Named Hurricane David, the storm reached speeds of up to 277 kph (172 mph), and lasted for two weeks. During that time, the island's coastlines were bombarded by huge waves, and 1,300 people lost their lives.

Flood waters produced by Hurricane Hugo in 1989 swept this boat from its harbour mooring to a nearby golf course. Hugo hit the Virgin Islands first. It then moved over warm water, where it gained more energy, and then struck South Carolina, in the USA.

A low, flat, and well-secured roof helped this house to survive almost entirely intact

REDUCED TO RUBBLE
In April 1991, a hurricane called Cyclone 2B crept up the Bay of Bengal and wreaked havoc on the people of Bangladesh. The storm brought with it 240-kph (150-mph) winds and a ferocious 6-m (20-ft) tidal wave. The winds reduced thousands of homes to rubble, while floods claimed the lives of over 140,000 people.

WAVE POWER
Vast areas of the US were flooded when Hurricane Floyd struck in 1999. At the centre of every hurricane is a swell, or bulge, of water up to 3 m (10 ft) high. This is because the atmospheric pressure at the heart of a hurricane is very low. If a hurricane moves close to land, the swell becomes a wave that can cause flooding, crop damage, and loss of life.

I WILL SURVIVE
In August 1992, Hurricane Andrew caused extensive damage throughout the Bahamas, Louisiana, and Florida in the USA. The hurricane caused 52 deaths and about $22 billion in damage. It ravaged many towns, and left thousands of people homeless. The lucky resident of this house in Florida, however, was proud to have lived through the fierce storms.

WITHOUT WARNING
In late December 1974, Cyclone Tracy formed 500 km (310 miles) northeast of the Australian coast. The local Tropical Cyclone Warning Centre tracked the storm – it seemed that the hurricane would miss land. Unexpectedly, in the early hours of Christmas Day, it turned and approached the town of Darwin. About 90 per cent of the town's buildings were destroyed, leaving half of its 40,000 residents homeless. Within a week of the disaster, over 20,000 people had been airlifted to other parts of the country.

Fog and smog

WHEN THE AIR IS FULL of moisture and the temperature drops, fog may occur. Fog is simply cloud at ground level. It consists of countless tiny droplets of water suspended in the air. Light passing through fog scatters in every direction, making it translucent, like tracing paper. In thick fog, visibility can be reduced to less than a few metres. Travel in these conditions is treacherous and accidents on the roads, at sea, or in the air are common. Not much can be done to reduce the danger, but foghorns or radar can locate ships and aeroplanes, and lighthouses and traffic signals can help to guide them to safety. Fog costs airlines millions of pounds each year through airport shutdowns. When fog combines with smoke, a thick and dangerous mixture, called smog, may form.

PEA-SOUPER
Until the 1960s, London, England, suffered frequent and serious smog caused by the burning of coal. These smogs, nicknamed "pea-soupers", caused serious, and often fatal, respiratory (breathing) problems. The city was cured of this problem by The Clean Air Acts of 1956 and 1968, which forced people to use "smokeless fuel".

CLEAR FOR TAKE-OFF
During World War II, a method was devised to clear fog from airport runways. Huge amounts of kerosene were burned to provide heat. The heat turned the water droplets in the fog into invisible vapour. This method was successful, but is seldom used today, because it is very expensive and can be dangerous.

Member of airport staff ignites fog burners

WATER CATCHERS
For residents of Chungungo village, Chile, frequent fog is actually a blessing. These long plastic fences just outside the village catch water from fog that blows in from the sea. Chungungo lies in a very dry location, and the water that the fences collect provides much of the village's water supply.

Sulphurous fog hangs over Christchurch in New Zealand

CLEANING UP THE AIR
Sulphurous smog hangs in the air above many towns and cities. This type of smog is produced when smoke from burning fuels combines with fog. On calm days, smog may linger for many hours, endangering health and proving treacherous to traffic. Nowadays, sulphurous smogs are less common due to city dwellers burning cleaner fuels. But equally deadly is "photochemical smog" caused by sunlight combining with air-pollutants.

Gas container

Loud noise travels through this horn

SOUNDING THE ALARM
Thick sea-fog can be hazardous to sailors. Gas released through the nozzle of this foghorn makes a very loud noise that can be heard clearly through the fog. This gives other sailors a chance to avoid a possible collision with a vessel that they cannot yet see. Large ships have huge, deafening foghorns that can be heard over many kilometres.

LIGHTING THE WAY
Before the invention of radar, sailors had no way of seeing ahead of them in thick sea-fogs. Lighthouses, like this one at the George Washington Bridge in New York, USA, gave sailors plenty of warning of the dangers ahead. By flashing a powerful beam of light during fogs and at night, lighthouses guided ships away from rocks or shallow water.

Golden Gate Bridge in San Francisco, USA, is hidden beneath a blanket of fog

FOGTOWN
San Francisco in the USA is sometimes referred to as "Fog City". The city is famous for its summer fog, which occurs when warm, moist air meets the cool water that travels into San Francisco Bay from further down the coast. This chilly fog normally lingers until about midday.

33

High seas

THE SEA COVERS about two-thirds of our planet. Strong winds constantly disturb the surface of the oceans, producing waves that break as they reach the shore. During severe storms, particularly hurricanes, sea water can cause widespread flooding. Many scientists fear that global warming will cause more of the ice-caps to melt resulting in an overall rise in sea levels. This threatens to increase the risk of serious flooding during storms at high tide in many coastal locations. But it is not only on the coast that people are at risk. Ships can sink in stormy weather, leaving passengers stranded in dangerous waters. Neither is it only people and their properties that are at risk from the sea – waves are continuously eroding the coastline.

IN DEEP WATER
High seas are normally stormy seas, with dangerous waves that can sink a ship or leave it stranded. Air-sea rescue helicopters rush to the aid of survivors. The helicopters hover above the sea while a rescuer is lowered on a winch to lift the survivors clear of the water.

A rescuer is lowered to the sea by a search and rescue helicopter

Collapsed coastal road caused by wave erosion

TEARING ALONG
Crashing waves wreak havoc on coastlines. They dissolve pieces of rock and break off parts of cliffs. The stormier the sea, and the higher its level, the greater the erosion. If global warming continues, sea levels will rise, increasing the rate of erosion and the risk of flooding.

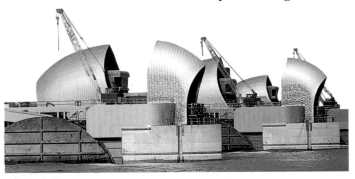

HOLDING BACK
The Thames River Barrier in London, UK, aims to protect the city from flooding until at least 2050. As sea levels rise, the threat of flooding in southern England is increasing. Ten huge gates can be raised when sea levels surge. These gates prevent water from travelling up the river towards London.

UNWELCOME VISITOR
This devastation on Okushiri Island, Japan, was caused by a huge, powerful wave called a tsunami. Tsunamis, often mistakenly called tidal waves, are triggered by vibrations from earthquakes beneath the seabed.

STORMY SEA
When Hurricane Hugo hit the West Indies and southeastern USA in 1989, it produced a surge 2 m (6 ft) high in open water. This rose to 6 m (18 ft) in some places, where the water was funnelled up along valleys. The sudden and dramatic surge in sea level when a hurricane reaches land is caused by low air pressure at the storm's centre.

WALL OF WATER
An ocean wave begins as wind blows across the sea's surface, making the water swing up and down, and back and forth. When waves approach the shore, where the sea becomes shallower, they move more slowly, and their crests become taller and closer together. Eventually the crests overtake the slower water at the base and the waves topple over, forming breakers.

This huge plunging wave is on the verge of breaking

Snowstorms

EXTREMELY COLD CONDITIONS can endanger the lives of people and animals. A heavy snowfall can make roads impassable or bury buildings, particularly when the wind blows the snow into piles, called snowdrifts. Snow and strong winds cause blizzards, which reduce visibility, and make travel by road treacherous. When the temperature falls below freezing point – 0°C (32°F) – snow will settle on the ground. Snowflakes are clumps of tiny ice crystals produced inside a cloud. These crystals form as water vapour freezes around tiny specks of mineral dust in the atmosphere. Ice storms occur when water in the air freezes to form icy fog at ground level. Everything becomes coated in an icy layer. The ice can become so thick that trees collapse under the weight.

PILED HIGH
Snow has piled up against the side of this house in Derbyshire, England, obscuring ground-floor windows and making it difficult to reach the front door. Snowdrifts, such as this, form when snow carried by the wind is stopped in its tracks by an obstacle.

Ice crystal from a snowflake

WHAT IS SNOW?
The ice crystals that make up snowflakes are too small to see with the naked eye. Their beautiful symmetrical shapes can, however, be viewed through a microscope. No two snowflakes are the same because their growth within a cloud depends on temperature, humidity, and air currents. These conditions are never identical for any two snowflakes.

WHITE-OUT
Blizzard conditions have forced these drivers to stop their cars. If they remain in their vehicles, they can be found more easily, but they may find warmth and shelter if there are houses or other buildings nearby. One person froze to death during this particular snowstorm, near Caen in France.

Blade of a snowplough clearing a road in France

CLEARING THE WAY
In areas where heavy snow is common, snowploughs keep major roads clear. Drivers use tyre chains for a better grip. But for unprepared communities, a sudden snowfall can cause chaos. Tyres easily lose their grip and accidents are common.

FROZEN DRIPS

Icicles are a common sight on very cold days. They form as water drips from ridges, such as rooftops or the branches of trees. The drips do not freeze all at once. Instead, only a small amount freezes, while the rest drips off. Part of the next drip freezes, too, and gradually an icicle builds up.

WIND CHILL

This man's face-warmer froze as he shovelled snow outside his home in Milwaukee, Wisconsin, USA. The temperature during this severe winter storm, in December 1995, was -35°C (-30°F), but the "wind chill" made it feel like -70°C (-90°F). Wind chill occurs on a windy day, when heat passes from your warm body to cold air more quickly than on a calm day, making the temperature feel even lower than it is in reality. Wearing several layers of clothing, covering as much of your body as possible, is the best way to keep warm, and prevent frostbite.

Icicles hang from a cliff during an ice storm in Arizona, USA

STAYING INDOORS

Extreme cold weather can close down schools and businesses, and force people to stay indoors for safety and warmth. Vehicles may become frozen solid and aeroplanes may be unable to take off due to ice on the wings. This car was covered in a sheet of ice during a severe winter storm in northeast Canada, when the temperature dropped to -29°C (-20°F). During the storm, trees fell down under the weight of ice, and tens of thousands of cattle froze to death.

AVALANCHE HAZARD — RISQUE D'AVALANCHE
MODERATE
MODÉRÉ
LOW HIGH
BAS ÉLEVÉ
EXTREME
EXTRÊME
INFORMATION   RENSEIGNEMENTS

WATCHING FOR SIGNS
Most mountain resorts have some way of alerting people to avalanche danger. Although difficult to predict exactly where and when an avalanche will strike, by examining the snow, experts can tell when an area is at risk.

Avalanche

ONE OF THE MOST TERRIFYING and dangerous things that can happen in mountainous areas is an avalanche – when huge amounts of snow slide down a mountain slope. A major avalanche can bury buildings – and the people in them. The Swiss Alps, with its numerous ski resorts, is one of the areas most at risk – every year, there are about 10,000 avalanches in that region. Avalanches occur after heavy snowfall has caused snow to build up on mountain slopes. Snow collects in layers – a new one laid during each snowfall. When an avalanche is imminent – when the snow layers are unstable – it can be triggered by strong winds, changes in temperature, or vibrations. Barriers are sometimes built to protect roads or villages, but little can be done to stop the hundreds, or even thousands, of tonnes of snow that tumble down a mountain during a large avalanche. It is important that anybody caught under this cold, heavy blanket is rescued as quickly as possible.

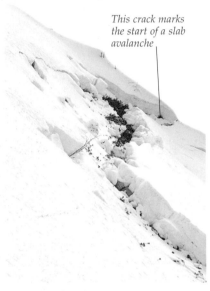

This crack marks the start of a slab avalanche

BREAKING AWAY
Most avalanches occur when melted snow breaks away as large slabs from the rock below. As a slab begins to move, large cracks, called fissures, appear in the snow. These cracks most often appear on bulging slopes and on cornices (slabs of snow that overhang cliff tops).

UNDER COVER
In areas where avalanches are common, protective sheds are often built over major roads. The sheds allow avalanches to pass over the road. Without these constructions, some roads would be blocked for much of the year.

Snow fences protect mountain villages in Switzerland

SNOW STOPPERS
Sturdy trees growing on a mountainside can absorb some of the energy of sliding snow. However, logging, acid rain, and increased tourism have dramatically reduced the number of trees in many mountain areas. Artificial barriers made of wood, concrete, or metal, can provide similar protection.

BANG, BANG
When a mass of snow is ready to become an avalanche, it can be set off by the slightest vibration. The best defence against potentially destructive avalanches is to trigger them before too much snow builds up. In places where the threat of serious avalanches is great, patrol teams use explosives to set them off deliberately.

LOOK CLOSELY
In regions prone to avalanches it is important to monitor the stability of the snow. Forecasters build snow pits so that they can examine the layers. An avalanche is more likely to occur if any of the layers contains air or is made up of graupel (ice pellets). These pellets can roll over each other allowing large slabs of snow above to break away.

An avalanche forecaster checks the stability of snow layers

RIVER OF SNOW
During this massive avalanche on Denali Peak, Alaska, tonnes of powdery, dry snow crashed to the valley floor. Airborne powder avalanches such as this occur soon after a fresh snowfall. They flow like liquid water, throwing up snow in vast splashes on reaching the valley floor. The high-speed mass of snow smothers everything in its path, and compresses the air in front of it creating loud tremors.

A rescue dog searches for survivors in the Swiss Alps

SNIFF SEARCH
Specially trained dogs help to locate people trapped under heavy snow after avalanches. With their highly developed sense of smell, dogs are still more efficient than any electronic sensor, although off-piste skiers do now carry personal radio beacons in case they are buried by an avalanche. The most famous breed of rescue dog – the Saint Bernard – was named after an 11th-century saint.

Floods and landslides

MORE THAN ONE-THIRD of all deaths from natural disasters are caused by flooding. A flash flood occurs when rain is very heavy and rivers break their banks, or sewers quickly become overwhelmed. More widespread devastation is caused by broadscale floods, in which water builds up over a period of weeks. In the Indian subcontinent, seasonal winds called monsoons bring torrential rain every summer. During severe floods, buildings are often ruined and people may drown. When torrential rain combines with high tides and strong winds, those living near a coastline are particularly at risk. Heavy rain can bring another problem – landslides. When large volumes of water mix with soil, the result is a thick liquid that can slip down a hillside, burying anything in its path.

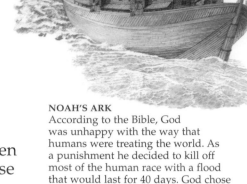

NOAH'S ARK
According to the Bible, God was unhappy with the way that humans were treating the world. As a punishment he decided to kill off most of the human race with a flood that would last for 40 days. God chose Noah and his family to survive the deluge. He instructed Noah to build an ark and carry with him a male and female from each of the Earth's species.

Damage caused by the Johnstown flash flood

DAM BUSTER
After heavy rain on 31 May 1889, a dam near Johnstown, Pennsylvania, USA, collapsed. Thousands of tonnes of water descended on to the town. The northern part of the city was swept away, and a total of 2,209 people died. The city was left with a huge clear-up operation.

DROWNED RICE
On the island of Java in Indonesia, monsoon rains are usually a blessing. Without these rains, vital rice crops would not survive. But sometimes, particularly heavy rains bring floods that endanger lives and precious crops.

A farmer in Java frantically tries to save a rice crop from flood-borne volcanic debris

BREAKING THE BANK
During the rainy monsoon season, the River Ganges in south Asia frequently bursts its banks. The floods of July and August 1998 were the worst in 20 years and left up to two-thirds of Bangladesh submerged. About 1,500 people died. Some victims drowned, but most died from snakebites or waterborne diseases, because medical assistance was unable to reach them.

MUDDY RIVER
Residents of Quindici in Italy fled their homes in May 1998, after two days of torrential rain. As local rivers burst their banks, muddy water poured through the town. The flood left over 3,000 people homeless and killed about 50 people – many of them buried under a thick layer of mud. The clean-up operation took more than three months.

Landslide debris on a 30-m (98-ft) high clay slope

WATERY INTRUDER
Storm waters broke through the windows of this seaside home in Florida, USA, during Hurricane Andrew in 1991. Hurricanes always bring fierce winds, and a surge of high water produced by the low atmospheric pressure at their centre.

MOVING MUD
When water and mud mix on a hillside, gravity pulls the mud and anything else in its path downwards. Part of this hotel in the coastal resort of Scarborough, England, slipped downhill during a landslide in June 1993.

STORM ON THE WATERFRONT
These residents of Florida Keys, USA, sought refuge as Hurricane George hit the coastline in 1998. They were forced to battle against 140-kph (90-mph) winds and a surge of water from the Atlantic Ocean. By the time the hurricane reached Florida, severe floods had killed hundreds and affected the lives of thousands of people in the Caribbean.

Home upturned by a powerful storm surge

Deadly droughts

Dᴇsᴇʀᴛs ᴀʀᴇ ᴘʟᴀᴄᴇs ᴏғ ᴘᴇʀᴍᴀɴᴇɴᴛ ᴅʀᴏᴜɢʜᴛ. Any region suffering from a lack of water caused by a lower-than-usual rainfall is said to be in drought. As rivers, lakes, and soil dry up, crops fail and animals starve to death. This can lead to widespread famine among humans. Advances in medicine, transport, and communications during the 20th century allowed aid agencies to lessen the effects of water scarcity. But droughts continue to be a severe problem in Ethiopia and other parts of Africa. Although a natural phenomenon, drought is sometimes caused by human activities. In the 1930s, for example, a huge area of the USA became known as the Dust Bowl due to over farming. In times of severe water shortage, efforts have been made to create rain clouds, but with limited success.

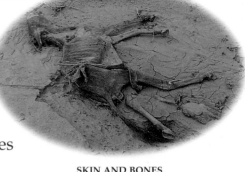

SKIN AND BONES
Animal carcasses are a common sight during severe droughts. This unfortunate animal dried out before it had a chance to decay.

POWERFUL PAINTING
This Australian Aboriginal bark painting comes from Arnhem Land – a hot, dry region of northern Australia. It was used in rain-making ceremonies, and the central image of a stingray symbolizes the "watery" power that summons the rain.

Animals gather around a waterhole in Namibia, Southern Africa

DIMINISHING SUPPLY
Animals in dry climates often gather around scarce pools of water, called waterholes. In times of drought, more water is lost from the waterhole – from evaporation and drinking – than is supplied by rainfall. There are fewer plants during a drought, too, so food supplies also dwindle. As a result, millions of animals can die during a severe drought.

WAR AND WANT
One of the worst droughts of recent times caused a terrible famine in Ethiopia during most of the 1980s. Seasonal droughts are fairly common in Ethiopia, but the civil war that was taking place there made the situation much worse. International aid agencies helped to keep many alive, but the death toll still exceeded 1.5 million people.

FIGHTING FIRE WITH FIRE
Forest fires are one disastrous consequence of drought. The dry leaves and wood of dead or dying trees and other plants provide excellent fuel for a raging fire. Most fires start naturally, but sometimes a careless act, such as a dropped match, can cause a forest fire in warm, dry territory. Some trees actually have bark that is fireproof or that peels off when it ignites. There are even trees that will not germinate until their cones are scorched.

BLOWING IN THE WIND

Most of the world's deserts are covered in sand or sandy soil. Because deserts are in permanent drought, most of the sand is normally dry. The wind can blow dry sand grains around, causing sandstorms that can be uncomfortable, or even dangerous, for people and animals. One result of sandstorms is sand dunes, which make up much of the landscape of the hottest deserts.

BLACK BLIZZARDS

During the 1930s, the Great Plains of the North American Midwest suffered from a long, severe drought. Grasses that usually protected the fields had been ploughed, so when drought struck, the topsoil dried to a dust and was blown away in huge black clouds. Thousands were driven from their homes, and some died of starvation or lung disease caused by inhaling the dust.

THIRSTY LEAVES

The kokerboom tree is found in the drylands of southwest Africa. It can survive several years of drought, during which time its leaves shrink, having lost most of their moisture.

CRACKING UP

Large areas of land with no vegetation can quickly suffer from drought. Plants help to reduce winds that can increase the rate of evaporation from the soil, and they also act as a store of water themselves. Water helps to bind together the grains that make up soil. This is why mud cracks up, becomes brittle, and produces dusty conditions when it is dry.

Lake Naivasha in Kenya, Africa, dried up by a drought

Polar extremes

THE NORTH AND SOUTH POLES are freezing cold all year round. This is because they receive less sunlight than the rest of the world. The area around the north pole, called the Arctic, has no land, only thick ice. Antarctica, around the south pole, has land that is covered by a permanent layer of snow. Winds can be very strong in Antarctica. They are produced as cold air flows off steep slopes into valleys or coastlines. The winds can blow snow into a blizzard that makes it difficult to see. During the long, dark polar winters, temperatures are rarely higher than -40°C (-40°F). The polar regions are much colder than the rest of the world, and play an important part in global weather. Water from the poles, for example, flows towards the equator, as deep, cold currents. These currents affect the weather in many parts of the world.

An icebreaker clears a path through the St Lawrence River, Canada

BREAKING THE ICE
Unlike pure water, salty sea water freezes a few degrees below 0°C (32°F). During winter, when huge amounts of sea ice form, it is important to keep waterways clear. Powerful ice-breaking ships transport vital supplies and also act as research stations.

EYE PROTECTION
Goggles protect eyes from the glare of sunlight, which is reflected by the snow. They also prevent too much heat loss.

ICE STATION
This research station in Antarctica is the temporary home to scientists from around the world. During the summer, nearly 4,000 people live and work at 42 polar sites. Fewer than 1,000 people live there in winter. By studying the weather at the poles, scientists can gain a more complete picture of the Earth's weather patterns.

GET A GRIP
Climbing boots can be specially adapted for icy conditions. A thermal lining helps to retain body heat. Crampons (spikes) can be attached to the soles to provide grip. Trousers can be clipped onto the boots to cover up the ankles.

Plastic outer layer is tough and durable

Bright red colour makes the jacket stand out in blizzard conditions

Elasticated cuffs keep out icy winds

Spikes help to grip thick, slippery ice

Salopettes

FLY THE FLAG
The snow that falls or is whipped up during a blizzard can bury important items. Some people plant coloured flags so that they can easily find their tents and supplies when the storm dies down.

Pyramid tent designed to withstand high-speed blizzard winds

WEATHER STATION
Automatic weather stations are positioned across the polar regions. Forecasting the weather is important for the safety of the scientists who live and work in these hostile environments.

Weather balloon for gathering data about the atmosphere

Undergarment traps a layer of air, which is warmed by the body

WEATHER BALLOON
Equipment is loaded into this weather balloon, which will measure the concentration of gases in the Antarctic atmosphere, as well as the temperature high in the air. These measurements can help scientists to test their theories of the weather, and make more accurate forecasts.

Waterproof nylon outer layer with goosedown stuffing

Scientists in Antarctica use a long, hollow drill to extract samples from the sea ice

FROZEN IN TIME
Much of the ice at the poles has been frozen for thousands or millions of years. The ice preserves things that were around at the time the ice formed. These include pollens, micro-organisms, dust from volcanoes and comets. By studying samples of melted ice, scientists can discover what the climate was like many years ago.

STAYING ALIVE
In polar climates, people protect their hands with thick, multi-layered gloves. Hands and feet are most at risk when temperatures fall below freezing. The body shuts off blood to these parts in an attempt to reduce heat loss. But severe conditions can cause frostbite.

WRAP UP
Polar scientists and explorers wear "extreme cold weather outfits". Outer layers consist of waterproof jacket and salopettes. They are made up of several layers of different materials, which is the best way to reduce heat loss. The most important thing is to cover as much of the body as possible – bare skin loses heat quickly in cold air.

Weather watch

WHEN A HURRICANE is about to hit, many deaths can be avoided if adequate warning is given. A hurricane can be tracked using weather satellites, but other types of extreme weather, such as drought or a local thunderstorm, are difficult to predict using observations from space. Instead, ground-based measurements – including wind speed, temperature, and atmospheric pressure – are necessary. The data are recorded using a variety of instruments located around the world, on land and at sea. Forecasters use powerful computers to analyze these recordings and to predict a few days in advance how the weather will behave. When bad weather is about to hit, warnings can be issued. The biggest challenges in forecasting are to predict short-lived phenomena such as tornadoes, and long-term conditions such as drought.

SIGNS FROM SPACE
Geostationary satellites, such as *Meteostat 4* (left), hover in space about 36,000 km (21,600 miles) above the equator. Day and night, these satellites record atmospheric temperatures and cloud patterns of a particular region.

Solar cells power the spacecraft

Radar gives a clear picture of clouds and rainfall

About 400 knobbly projections help to stabilize this balloon while in flight

Weather instruments are mounted here to give temperature and humidity readings

Doppler-radar dome

ROUND RADAR
Highly sensitive radar equipment enables weather scientists to make increasingly accurate forecasts. The US National Weather Service relies on a network of ground-based Doppler-radar stations to calculate cloud positions, and measure wind speeds and rainfall.

HIGH IN THE SKY
Balloons are an essential part of the world's weather forecasting system. They carry measuring equipment high up into the Earth's atmosphere and transmit readings by radio. This balloon records temperature and humidity. Wind speed can be calculated by using radar to track the balloon in flight. Measurements of conditions in the upper atmosphere are very important for predicting what the weather may do next, and for discovering more about how the weather works.

WORKING WITH THE WEATHER
Meteorologists based in research centres around the world use powerful computers to analyze weather measurements taken from land, sea, air, and space. Their findings help them to build a picture of the world's weather patterns. If forecasters predict hurricanes or other extreme weather, they issue warnings, or "watches", via the media.

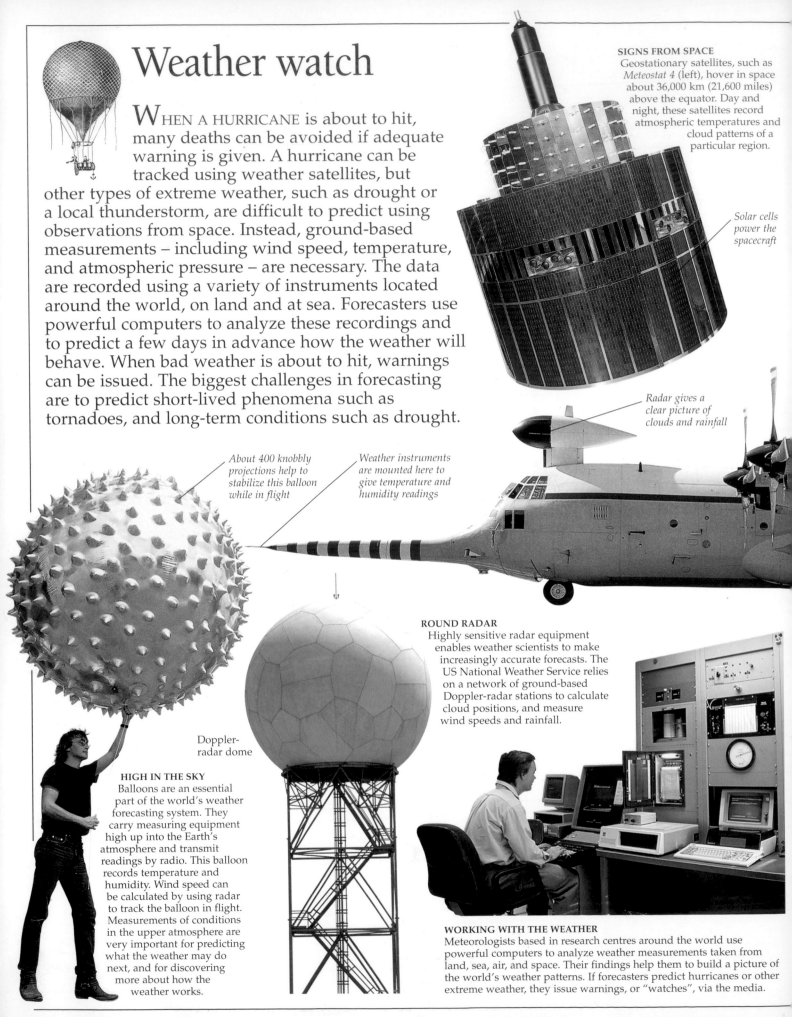

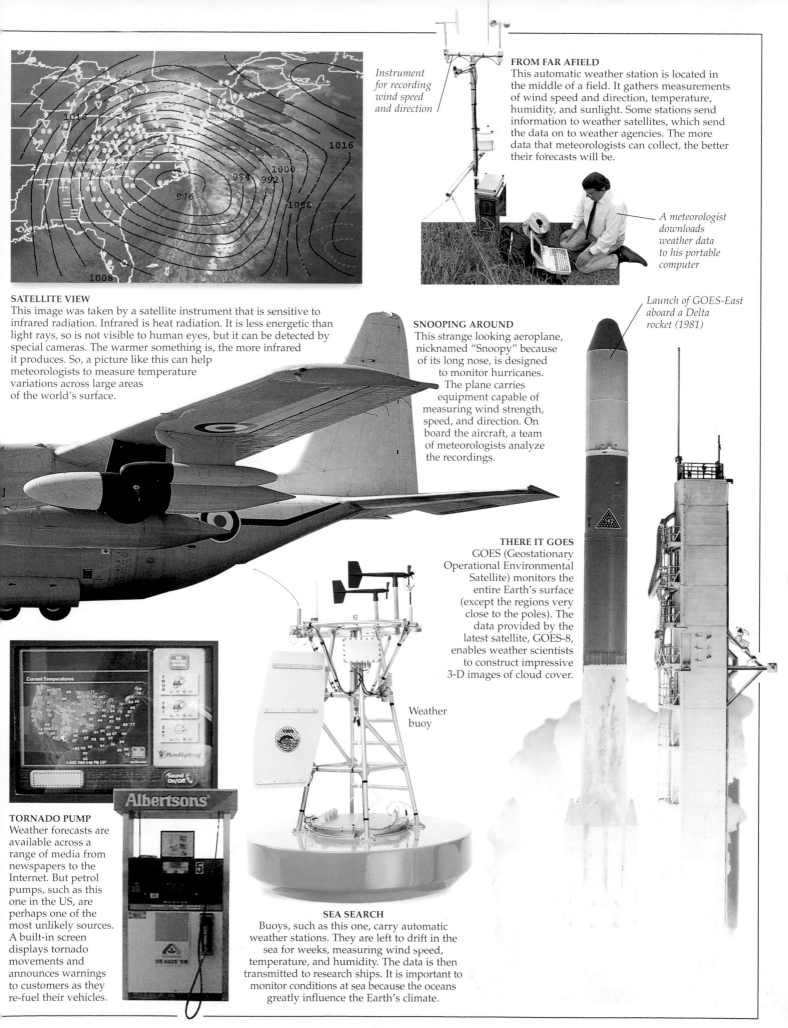

SATELLITE VIEW
This image was taken by a satellite instrument that is sensitive to infrared radiation. Infrared is heat radiation. It is less energetic than light rays, so is not visible to human eyes, but it can be detected by special cameras. The warmer something is, the more infrared it produces. So, a picture like this can help meteorologists to measure temperature variations across large areas of the world's surface.

Instrument for recording wind speed and direction

FROM FAR AFIELD
This automatic weather station is located in the middle of a field. It gathers measurements of wind speed and direction, temperature, humidity, and sunlight. Some stations send information to weather satellites, which send the data on to weather agencies. The more data that meteorologists can collect, the better their forecasts will be.

A meteorologist downloads weather data to his portable computer

Launch of GOES-East aboard a Delta rocket (1981)

SNOOPING AROUND
This strange looking aeroplane, nicknamed "Snoopy" because of its long nose, is designed to monitor hurricanes. The plane carries equipment capable of measuring wind strength, speed, and direction. On board the aircraft, a team of meteorologists analyze the recordings.

THERE IT GOES
GOES (Geostationary Operational Environmental Satellite) monitors the entire Earth's surface (except the regions very close to the poles). The data provided by the latest satellite, GOES-8, enables weather scientists to construct impressive 3-D images of cloud cover.

Weather buoy

TORNADO PUMP
Weather forecasts are available across a range of media from newspapers to the Internet. But petrol pumps, such as this one in the US, are perhaps one of the most unlikely sources. A built-in screen displays tornado movements and announces warnings to customers as they re-fuel their vehicles.

SEA SEARCH
Buoys, such as this one, carry automatic weather stations. They are left to drift in the sea for weeks, measuring wind speed, temperature, and humidity. The data is then transmitted to research ships. It is important to monitor conditions at sea because the oceans greatly influence the Earth's climate.

Disaster relief

NATURE CAN CAUSE DESTRUCTION on a huge scale through extreme weather phenomena such as storms, droughts, and floods. When it does, people's lives are dramatically affected, and they need help to keep them alive and well before conditions begin to return to normal. After a hurricane, for example, people may need medical care, or somewhere to stay while their homes are being cleared of floodwater, repaired, or even rebuilt. Food and water supplies may be affected, too. International aid agencies, such as the Red Cross, provide assistance to people who suffer at the hands of the weather. These agencies try to distribute food and medical supplies to wherever they are needed.

Clean-up operation following a tornado in Connecticut, USA, October 1979

UPTURNED LIVES
A rescuer searches the debris of this upturned home following a tornado in Florida, USA. People who live in southwestern USA have more than their fair share of hurricanes and tornadoes. But however often terrible weather occurs, they can never be fully prepared. Before rebuilding can begin, the inhabitants must be temporarily housed, perhaps in a local school or supermarket.

DAMAGE DEMOLITION
The building above was completely destroyed by a powerful tornado. Before it can be rebuilt, it needs to be completely demolished, with the help of this powerful digger. The governments of wealthy countries set aside emergency funds with which to pay for rebuilding work. Poorer countries must often rely on outside aid.

PORTABLE WATER
Even during a flood, fresh drinking water is often in short supply. This Filipino boy is collecting fresh water from a tank, because his water supply was cut off by flood damage.

Temporary water tank provides fresh water to flood victims

MOPPING UP
One of the main priorities in an area hit by flooding is to drain off the excess water. Emergency services use powerful pumps to clear the streets. Sandbags protect properties from floodwater, and also control the direction of the flow.

AIR MEALS

When any kind of natural disaster strikes a remote location, the quickest way to bring aid to the area is to drop supplies from the sky. The food carried by this aeroplane helped many people stay alive during a severe drought in Sudan, Africa. Each of the tightly bound parcels contained mostly flour, oil, and canned fruit. It is difficult to drop water in these parcels, even though it is often what is most needed.

*Makeshift shelters in a
refugee camp in Ethiopia*

TEMPORARY HOMES

When drought brought famine to Ethiopia in 1989, the United Nations set up this camp in Sidamo Province. Forty-five thousand people took refuge from the famine here. Each family was given some plastic sheeting to act as a temporary shelter, a sleeping mat, and cooking utensils, as well as food and water. Refugees had to find their own materials for cooking and for building huts, putting a great strain on scarce resources.

*Emergency
food supplies*

DISEASE PREVENTION

Epidemics can break out rapidly in disaster sites, and are a common cause of death. This aid worker is spraying insecticide to kill off disease-spreading mosquitoes, which thrive in murky floodwaters. Care must be taken to use insecticides that will not harm people when they filter into the water supply.

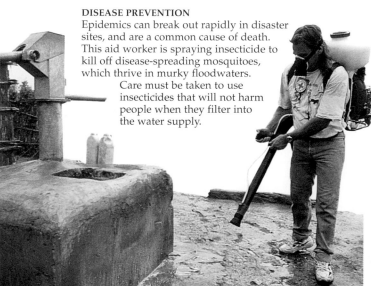

ALL DRIED UP

When this picture was taken, there had been no rain in the Suguta Valley, Kenya, for seven years. Famine is common during a serious drought, particularly in remote areas where it is difficult to obtain supplies. This is why food aid is important. Here, the food is being supplied by Oxfam, a charity that was set up to help fight against famine.

Nature's survivors

THE WORLD'S PLANTS AND ANIMALS are all well suited to their environments. If they were not, they would soon die out, particularly in extreme climates such as deserts. The plants and animals that live today are different from those of long ago. Some living things are so well adapted to their surroundings, in such strange ways, that you may think that they have been specially designed to live there. But living things adapt to their surroundings gradually – over many generations. Camels, for example, have developed the ability to overcome the scarcity of water in the desert. In dry places, plants retain as much water as they can. In rainy places, they are actually able to stop too much water from collecting on their leaves.

FEATHER COAT
Snowy owls live in Arctic regions. Their soft, fluffy feathers hold lots of air, which insulates their bodies against the harsh cold. Snowy owls even have feathers around their claws. If the weather becomes hot, these owls cannot take off their winter coats. They cool themselves by spreading their wings and panting.

FAT MONSTER
The gila monster is a lizard that lives in Mexico and the southwestern US. During the warm, rainy season, food – in the form of eggs, baby birds, and rodents – is plentiful, and the gila monster eats well. During this time, it stores body fat, on which it can live for long periods during the cold, dry winter.

Fat stored in the tail provides energy during the winter

UPSIDE-DOWN TREE
The strange-looking baobab tree is described in a myth. The story explains how the tree angered the gods by complaining. The gods punished the tree by uprooting it and re-planting it upside down. The real reason for the tree's odd appearance is that it only has leaves for up to three months per year. This, together with the tree's store of water in its huge trunk, help to enable the tree to survive the dry season in its native East Africa.

Drip tip of a rainforest leaf

USEFUL TIPS
In a rainforest, it is not unusual for about 1 m (3 ft) of rain to fall each month during the rainy season. Plants depend on water to survive, but if their leaves were constantly coated with a layer of water, they would die. So, some rainforest leaves have developed pointed "drip tips", to carry the water away.

STEMMING THE FLOW
A plant's leaves are covered with tiny holes, called stomata, that allow water to escape. As water evaporates through the stomata, more is drawn up through the plant from the soil. Where water is scarce, such as in the desert, plants usually have fewer or smaller leaves. Many cacti, such as this hedgehog cactus, have no leaves at all. These plants are just large water-holding stems.

SOME LIKE IT WET
Red-eyed tree frogs are well adapted to life in the rainforest. They have suckers on their feet that help them to clamber among the branches. Like all frogs, tree frogs have moist skin. If their skin dries out, they will die. So, far from being under threat from the heavy rainfall in the rainforest, tree frogs thrive in their damp environment.

UNDERGROUND MOVEMENT
Most amphibians have a slimy skin, which must remain moist at all times. During times of drought, many amphibians remain in burrows or gather together in a moist location, such as a rotting log. In countries with a dry season, some frogs become totally dormant when water supplies are low, surrounding themselves in a moist mud cocoon.

Australian burrowing frog

WATER FACTORY
Like many other animals that live in the constant drought of the desert, the camel can actually make water from its own body fat. A camel can use a quarter of its body weight to stay alive, without suffering any ill effects.

A camel can drink the equivalent of a bath full of water in just a few minutes

Overlapping feathers are closely packed to keep out fierce winds

IN A COLD CLIMATE
One of the few animals to live in the harsh conditions of the Antarctic all year round is the Emperor penguin. With waterproof feathers and thick fat layers under the skin, the penguins are perfectly adapted for survival on land and in the icy seas. During the winter, when male penguins tend the eggs and young, they are unable to swim off in search of food. At these times, their body fat provides an essential source of energy.

Fluffy-feathered chicks huddle together for warmth

Feet are small to minimize heat loss

Climate change

THE CLIMATE OF A PARTICULAR REGION is the typical weather in that area over the last 30 years. But climates can change. There are, for example, several known periods in history when temperatures across the world were much lower than they are now. During these "ice ages", more of the oceans' water froze, and the polar ice-caps grew larger. Ice also covered more land, in the form of huge glaciers. One of the causes of ice ages is the variation in the distance between the Earth and the sun. Some scientists believe that huge meteorite impacts are also sometimes to blame. At other times in the Earth's history, higher than normal temperatures have wiped out civilizations. Scientists use many techniques, including examining fossils or tree rings, to "read" climate records.

EVER-CHANGING SEA
The ammonoid, or ammonite, was a shelled marine animal that lived in warm oceans until about 66 million years ago. But ammonoid fossils have been found in the rocks under the oceans of Antarctica. Because Antarctica was not always at the south pole, it was not always cold. Like all continents, Antarctica has drifted thousands of kilometres over millions of years.

Frost fair on the Thames River in London, 1813

LOST CIVILIZATION
Dramatic changes in the climate can force people to move from their homes, and can even cause the end of civilizations. The Anasazi civilization lived in these caves, in the southwest of what is now the USA, until about 1280. They were forced to move away by a drought that lasted for about 23 years.

MINI ICE AGE
Between about 1500 and 1850, much of Europe experienced what is referred to as the "Little Ice Age". The average temperature was only a few degrees lower than normal, but this was enough to freeze huge amounts of sea water. Winters were very harsh, and rivers often froze over.

Thick, woolly coat provides insulation

Huge curved ivory tusks were used to ward off predators, and probably to sweep aside snow when feeding on grassy plains

COLD-CLIMATE ELEPHANT
During the last Great Ice Age, woolly mammoths lived in the icy tundra regions of North America, Europe, and Asia. Mammoths died out about 10,000 years ago, as the world's climate began to warm up.

Hair-covered trunk to keep out the cold

TREE CIRCLES

Trees grow thicker with each year they are alive. New living wood is created in a layer beneath the bark. Each year's growth appears as a ring. The warmer the climate is in a particular year, the more growth that occurs, and the thicker the ring becomes. By analyzing the width of tree rings, scientists can calculate the average temperatures for each year of the tree's life.

The thicker a tree ring, the warmer the climate in that year

Bristlecone pines growing on the White Mountains, California, USA

LIVING CLIMATE RECORD

The oldest living trees are bristlecone pines found in California and Nevada, USA. Some of these trees are over 4,000 years old, and are a living record of the history of the climate. The tree rings can be analyzed by boring into the trunk and removing a long thin sample of wood.

SPACE DUST

This crater, in what is now Arizona, USA, records the impact of a huge meteorite that hit the Earth 50,000 years ago. Millions of tonnes of dust were thrown up into the air, and most of it stayed in the air for about a year. The dust reflected much of the sun's light back into space. Some scientists believe that the dust from meteor impacts can cause reduced global temperatures.

MELTING FUTURE?

The world's average temperature is rising slowly – this is called global warming. Some scientists blame human activity, such as the burning of fuels, for some of this temperature increase. If global warming continues at its present rate, more and more of the ice at the north and south poles will melt causing flooding in many parts of the world during the next century.

A massive iceberg in Greenland dwarfs a passing fishing trawler

El Niño phenomenon

EVERY TWO TO TEN YEARS, part of the Pacific Ocean, near to the coast of South America, becomes warmer during winter than normal. Pacific winds change direction, blowing warm water eastwards towards South America. This phenomenon – known as El Niño – causes extreme weather throughout the tropics, and can last up to four years. Countries as far apart as Australia and Africa may suffer disruption to their normal rainfall patterns, which can result in severe flooding or drought. El Niño can also affect weather further afield than the tropics. It can cause average winter temperatures over North America to fall, and can increase winter rainfall over northwestern Europe. As El Niño can be predicted several months ahead, meteorologists are able to issue early warnings. These can allow farmers to alter their crops to suit the forecast conditions.

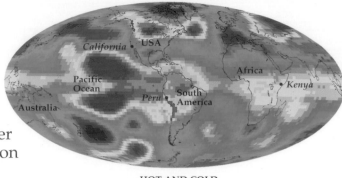

HOT AND COLD
This map of the Earth has been put together using information from satellites. It shows how the temperatures across the world were affected during an El Niño in 1983. The orange and red areas show warmer than normal temperatures, the blue areas are cooler than normal. The large red and orange patch over the eastern Pacific Ocean is due to El Niño.

HARD TIMES
El Niño (Spanish for "the Christ child") was given its name by Peruvian fishermen, because it appears around Christmas time. When El Niño winds blow warm water over the cool Peruvian seas, large numbers of fish disappear. This is because the plankton on which the fish feed cannot grow in warmer waters. Many Peruvians, whose livelihoods and survival depend on fishing, also suffer terribly at the hands of El Niño.

ON THE ROCKS
Sea lions and seabirds off the western coast of South America often die from starvation during an El Niño. They depend on the fish that thrive on the plankton in the normally cool waters. When El Niño hits, the cooler waters are pushed downwards, and the fish swim deeper – out of reach of the sea lions and seabirds.

WARM AND WET
During the 1998 El Niño, floods in Kenya, Africa, ruined maize crops, and spread diseases such as malaria. Kenya normally has low rainfall, but during an El Niño, warmer water mixes with the waters off the Kenyan coast. The subsequent increase in rainfall often causes flooding.

HEAVY SNOW
Changes in currents in the Pacific Ocean during an El Niño often affect the west coast of the USA. While some areas suffer from floods, other parts become much colder. For example, the El Niño of 1997–1998 brought much higher than normal snow levels to the mountains of southern California, USA.

SEABED SKELETONS
Bleached coral is a reliable indicator of the presence of an El Niño. Tiny colourful plants, called algae, live on coral, and are vital to its survival. They move away when the sea's temperature rises, leaving behind the coral's white "skeleton". In areas where temperatures are higher than normal, rich coral reefs become pale and barren as they die.

DROUGHT ALERT
El Niño reduces rainfall in Brazil, which sometimes leads to drought. During the El Niño of 1987, Brazil's grain production fell by 80 per cent. In 1992, however, scientists were able to predict the onset of El Niño. Farmers planted crops that would survive a drought, and the resulting harvest was only slightly less than normal.

BURNING UP
In 1998, El Niño brought drought to Sumatra, Indonesia. The drought had made the trees very dry and forest fires burned out of control. The fires burned for weeks, and covered Sumatra with thick smoke. It became so dark that drivers had to use their headlights during the day.

ALL DRIED UP
During an El Niño, winds push warm water eastwards towards South America, and away from Australia in the west. The cooler waters around eastern Australia lead to reduced rainfall, and large areas suffer from drought. During 1997, warnings of the approaching El Niño caused many Australian farmers to abandon their land.

WASHED AWAY
Much of the west coast of Peru and Chile, in South America, is very dry, because the coastal waters there are normally cool. During an El Niño in February 1998, however, rain began to fall at an incredible rate – up to 15 cm (6 in) every day. The floods that resulted broke river banks, and in some cases swept away whole villages.

Freaky conditions

THE EARTH'S ATMOSPHERE, together with the sun, provides all the weather conditions experienced on Earth. For example, the sun's energy evaporates water into the atmosphere, to produce clouds. Most people experience sunshine, wind, rain, and perhaps snow at some time, but the sun and the atmosphere can also create strange conditions. Many people have seen a rainbow, caused by sunlight hitting raindrops and bouncing back; but few have seen a moonbow. Other tricks of light include haloes, mirages, and the spooky Brocken Spectre. Electricity in thunderclouds can also produce strange effects other than lightning, such as St Elmo's Fire. Electric charge is also responsible for the beautiful aurora lights. Some of the world's rarest and most strange phenomena remain unexplained.

MYSTERIOUS GLOW
One eerie effect of an electrified thundercloud is St Elmo's Fire. This is a rare bluish-green light that glows at the tips of pointed objects, such as a ship's rigging, during a storm. An object may glow in this way as it slowly leaks an electric charge that is in turn attracted to the charge at the base of a thundercloud.

A GHOSTLY SIGHT
Sometimes, climbers on high mountains see huge human figures before them. This effect is called the Brocken Spectre, after the Brocken peak in Germany, where the phenomenon has been most famously reported. The figures are simply the climbers' own shadows cast on the bases of nearby clouds Sometimes, the shadows are surrounded by colourful haloes called Brocken Bows.

COLOURS IN THE SKY
When the sun is fairly low in the sky behind you, and it is raining, you may see a rainbow. Light from the sun reflects off the inside surfaces of raindrops, and bends as it travels through them. Each of the colours that make up sunlight is bent to a different angle, which is why a rainbow appears as a band of colours.

COLOURS AT MOONRISE
Just after the rising of a bright full moon in the east, shortly after the sun sets in the west, you may be lucky enough to see a moonbow. This is formed in the same way as a normal rainbow, so you must have the moon behind you and it must also be raining in the west. Moonbows are very rare.

GLOWING GLOBES
Thousands of people worldwide have reported seeing balls of light that either hover in midair or drift along before exploding violently or fading away. This effect, called ball lightning, is most likely an electrical phenomenon caused by thunderstorms.

As the hollow cylinder of snow moves it gathers more snow on the outside

MAGICAL SNOWBALLS
Snow sometimes plays a clever trick by rolling itself up just like a sleeping bag. This only happens when new snow falls on old and is blown by a strong warm wind. Although it is rare to see them forming, on a good day you may find a whole field full of spontaneous snowballs.

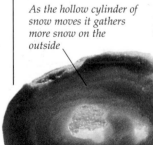

Rock reflected in the sand gives the illusion of water

DISTORTED VIEW
Reports of shimmering reflections in the desert and ships hanging upside down above the horizon at sea have been recorded for centuries. These are not pure fantasy, but refer to mirages, which are produced when light from distant objects bends as it passes through air at different temperatures.

SUN HALO

When sunlight passes through cirrus, or high-altitude clouds, a halo can be seen around the sun. Since ancient times, some people have believed haloes are a sign of imminent rain. This is one piece of weather folklore that has some truth to it – the presence of cirrus clouds does often precede rainfall.

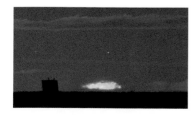

SUNSET SPARK

Occasionally, on clear days, just as the sun is setting or rising, a mysterious green flash lights up the sky. This effect is only visible over a definite horizon, such as the one at sea. The flashes are caused by sunlight being bent and scattered by dust particles in the atmosphere.

AURORAS

Spectacular displays of coloured light called auroras can often be seen near the Earth's north and south poles, and sometimes from farther afield. The light is produced high in the atmosphere as electrically charged solar particles are attracted towards the magnetic poles, and collide with air molecules.

Weather beyond Earth

THE SUN IS A STAR that sits at the centre of our solar system, and is orbited by nine planets and their moons. The sun's radiation causes weather on Earth by heating the atmosphere. Without an atmosphere, a planet can have no wind, rain, or snow. Mercury and many of the planets' moons – including Earth's moon – have virtually no atmosphere at all. The planets Venus and Mars do have atmospheres, and some of their weather is similar to Earth. Both planets have clouds and extreme winds, for example. Beyond Mars are the "gas giants" – Jupiter, Saturn, Uranus, and Neptune – which are huge balls of gas, with a small liquid or rocky core. The gases that make up these planets swirl around as the planets spin, forming spiral storms similar to hurricanes on Earth. Further from the sun than the gas giants is the tiny planet Pluto, where it is too cold for an atmosphere to form.

BLUE NEPTUNE
Neptune's winds blow as fast as 2,500 kph (1,575 mph), and are the strongest winds in the solar system. The planet appears blue because the atmosphere contains methane gas. The white cloud bands (above) are probably made of frozen methane, which cools as it rises.

The sky on Mars is pink during the day

The sun is more than 100 times larger than Earth

DUST STORM
Mars is covered by a layer of dust that contains iron oxide – a compound in rust – which gives the planet its reddish colour. Although the atmosphere on Mars is much thinner than on Earth, Mars does have fierce winds that blow huge amounts of dust across the planet's surface.

VENUSIAN VOLCANOES
The surface of Venus has many features that are similar to those found on Earth. There are volcanoes, for example, although most have been inactive for millions of years. Like the volcanoes on Earth, when those on Venus erupted they contributed gases to the atmosphere, which play a part in the planet's weather.

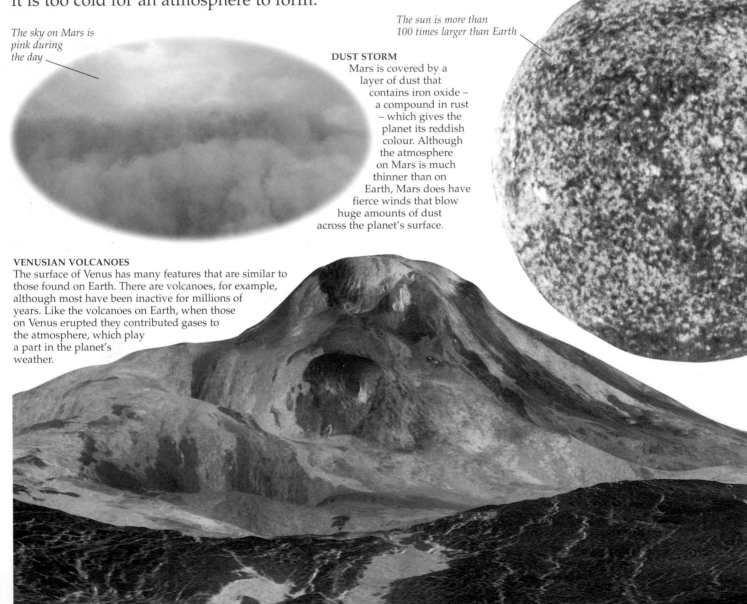

RUNNING RINGS

You can identify the planet Saturn – the second largest in the solar system – by its prominent rings. Like all the gas giants, Saturn is nearly all atmosphere, and becomes more and more dense the further towards the centre you go. The planet is warmed by the sun, but in some places, the outer atmosphere is still a chilly -190°C (-310°F).

Superbolt lightning storm

High-powered winds of up to 1,800 kph (1,118 mph) encircle Saturn

SCORCHING STORM

The sun is a ball of extremely hot gas. The surface is much cooler than the centre, but at more than 5,000°C (10,000°F), it is still hot enough to vaporize diamonds. The surface is a turbulent place, too. Huge storms, called prominences, caused by the sun's strong magnetic field, throw millions of tonnes of searing hot gas into space.

Storm prominence erupts on the sun

Ultraviolet image of the sun

SPINNING SPOTS

Jupiter – the largest of all the planets – spins rapidly. It takes less than ten hours to make one rotation. This movement causes the planet's atmosphere to swirl around, and is responsible for the Great Red Spot (above). This spot is a storm similar to a hurricane, but about twice the size of Earth. Jupiter's great storm has been raging for at least 330 years, since it was first observed.

CHARGED UP

Lightning on Earth is caused by updraughts of air in huge thunderclouds. Other planets have lightning, too, produced in the same way. Jupiter has particularly energetic lightning storms at its magnetic poles, which is thought to be caused partly by the planet's strong magnetic field.

Sulphuric cloud bands

Europa's icy surface

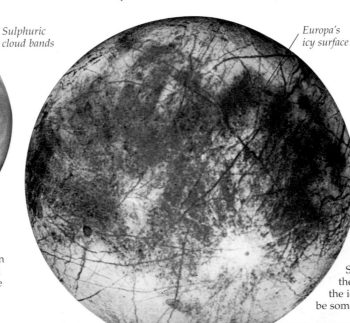

ICY EUROPA

One of Jupiter's moons, Europa, has a thin atmosphere made up largely of oxygen. It is a rocky ball coated in a layer of smooth water ice, which appears to be similar to pack-ice on Earth. Some space scientists think that there may be liquid water beneath the ice. If this is true then there could be some form of life in Europa's seas.

MOLTEN VENUS

With a surface temperature hot enough to melt lead, Venus is the hottest planet in the solar system. The planet is shrouded in thick clouds of sulphuric acid, and the atmospheric pressure at its surface is 90 times higher than that on Earth.

Did you know?

AMAZING FACTS

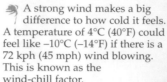

There is so much snow in Greenland that the Greenlanders have about 50 different words for snow, such as "aput" (snow on the ground) and "nittaalaq" (air thick with snow).

There are more than 8 million flashes of lightning every day.

Cumulonimbus clouds can be 11 km (7 miles) tall.

The air rises quickly through the tall cloud

A cumulonimbus cloud

Snow takes up much more room than rain. Sixty centimetres (24 in) of dry snow is roughly equivalent to 2.5 cm (1 in) of rain.

On 14 August 1979, a rainbow was visible in North Wales for three hours.

You can rarely hear thunder more than 10 km (6 miles) away from a storm, but you can see lightning at a distance of 100 km (60 miles) or more.

A strong wind makes a big difference to how cold it feels. A temperature of 4°C (40°F) could feel like −10°C (−14°F) if there is a 72 kph (45 mph) wind blowing. This is known as the wind-chill factor.

In storms, objects can be picked up whole and transported some distance before being dropped down again. Frogs have been whisked up in this way and dropped with the rain.

Warm air and rain thaw large quantities of snow more quickly than sunshine, because a lot of the sunshine is reflected by the snow.

Since 1979, when meteorologists started calling hurricanes by male and female names, "male" storms have caused four times as much damage as "female" storms.

Between 1995 and 2000, there was more hurricane activity in the North Atlantic than at any other period on record.

Permanent snow and ice together cover approximately 12 per cent of the Earth's land surface.

A lightning flash moves from the ground to the cloud. It moves at a speed of 37,000 km/second (22,992 miles/second).

Keriche, in Kenya, receives on average more hail than any other place on Earth, with hail falling on 132 days each year.

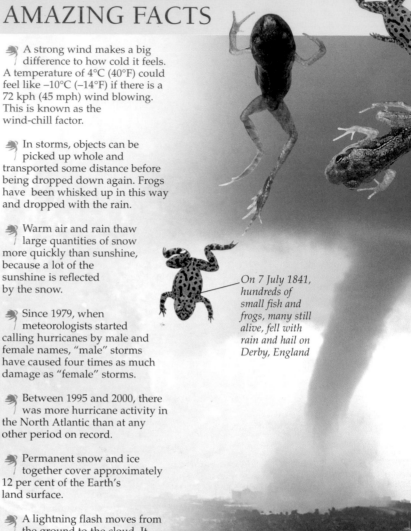

On 7 July 1841, hundreds of small fish and frogs, many still alive, fell with rain and hail on Derby, England

A tornado funnel sweeps across the ground

A park ranger called Roy Sullivan suffered seven lightning strikes over a period of 41 years. The lightning knocked him unconscious, set his hair on fire, and injured his chest and stomach.

Lightning can travel over 10 km (6 miles). So you can suffer a lightning strike even when there does not seem to be a storm overhead.

Dramatic high tides result partly from the high winds of an offshore storm, but also from low atmospheric pressure. A fall in pressure of one millibar causes the sea to rise by one centimetre, so a deep depression can cause a 70-cm (28-in) rise.

A single thunderstorm can drop as much as 500 million litres (110 million gallons) of rain.

Fork lightning

QUESTIONS AND ANSWERS

The aurora borealis

Q What causes the lights known as auroras?

A The solar wind is a stream of particles flowing from the polar regions of the sun. The Earth's magnetic shield protects us from this wind, but at the poles the particles create amazing light displays as they collide with molecules in the upper atmosphere. Near the north pole the lights are known as the aurora borealis, near the south pole they are called the aurora australis.

Q What is the blanket effect?

A At night, clouds reduce the heat that leaves the Earth, keeping the Earth warm. We call this the blanket effect.

Q What can happen where oceans meet?

A Where oceans meet, such as off the tips of South America and South Africa, storms create spectacular waves. At Cape Horn, the waves can be 20 m (65 ft) tall.

Q What are the doldrums?

A The doldrums are an almost windless region of rising hot air around the equator. The rising air currents form huge cumulonimbus clouds, which produce thunderstorms, and sometimes waterspouts.

Record Breakers

- The worst tornado outbreak in the world was in April 1974. In just 16 hours, 148 tornadoes struck 13 states, leaving 315 dead, 5,484 injured, and an incredible trail of destruction.

- The lowest recorded temperature in the world is -89.2°C (-129°F), taken at Vostok, Antarctica, on 21 July 1983.

- The wettest place in the world is Mawsynram in Meghalaya State, India, which has an average annual rainfall of 12,000 mm (472 in).

- The wettest day in the world was at Foc-Foc on the Ile de Reunion, in the Indian Ocean, where 1,825 mm (71 in) of rain fell in 24 hours.

- The windiest place in the world is Port Martin in Antarctica, where there are winds averaging more than 64 kph (40 mph) on at least 100 days each year.

- The greatest snowfall recorded in one day was at Silver Lake, Colorado, USA, on 14 April 1921, with a fall of 1.93 m (6 ft 4 in) of snow.

Ice crystals in a snowflake

A surfer enjoys South Africa's big waves

Timeline

HURRICANES, TORNADOES, and other forms of extreme weather have caused times of terrible suffering throughout history. This timeline charts some of the worst events over the past five centuries. Although we are now more knowledgeable about the causes of extreme weather and can predict the possible routes of storms and issue severe weather warnings, we cannot avoid the incredible destruction. Faced with the violence of a tropical cyclone or torrential flood, there is still relatively little we can do to protect ourselves.

Flooding on the plains of India

A ship from the Spanish Armada

- **1495** A hurricane strikes Christopher Columbus near Hispaniola.

- **1559** A hurricane sinks almost all of a Spanish fleet of 74 ships on their way to recapture Florida.

- **1588** A violent storm in the Bay of Biscay scatters the ships of the Spanish Armada as they set out in May to invade England. After refitting, the ships set off again in July.

- **1635** The Great Colonial Hurricane hits New England in August. It causes a 6-m (20-foot) tide in Boston, and destroys thousands of trees and houses.

- **1697** Lightning strikes a castle in Ireland, setting fire to the store of gunpowder and causing the castle to explode.

- **1776** A storm kills more than 6,000 on Martinique.

- **1780** The Great Hurricane, the deadliest in recorded history, leaves an estimated 22,000 dead in the Caribbean and destroys the British and French fleets.

- **1843** A violent hailstorm destroys crops and greenhouses in Norfolk, England.

- **1876–79** A prolonged, severe drought in northern China kills between nine and 13 million people.

- **1887** Between 900,000 and 2.5 million people die when the Yellow River floods an area of 26,000 sq km (10,000 sq miles) in China.

- **1888** A deadly hailstorm strikes Moradabad, northern India, killing 246 people. The hailstones are reported to be the size of cricket balls.

- **1900** In September, storm tides of 2.4– 4.5 m (8–15 ft) inundate Galveston Island, Texas, USA, killing more than 6,000 people.

- **1925** The Tri-State tornado causes an estimated 695 deaths in Missouri, Illinois, and Indiana, USA.

- **1928** The San Felipe hurricane kills 3,411 in the Caribbean and Florida, USA.

- **1930s** A drought in the North American Midwest turns vast areas of farmland into a desert known as the "Dust Bowl". Thousands die from heatstroke or breathing problems in the dust storms.

- **1930** A September hurricane leaves thousands dead in the Dominican Republic and almost totally destroys the capital, Santo Domingo.

A storm surge rushes ashore

- **1931** The Yangtze River floods large areas in China, destroying crops. About 3.7 million people perish in the floods and the resulting famine.

- **1953** A January storm surge of 2.5 m (8 ft) in Essex, England, and 4 m (13 ft) in parts of Holland, kills 300 people in England and about 1,800 in Holland. As a result, storm-surge barriers are constructed to protect vulnerable parts of Holland and eastern England.

- **1959** A hailstorm hits Selden, Kansas, USA, on 3 June. It causes $500,000 damage and buries an area 15 km by 10 km (9 miles by 6 miles) in hailstones to a depth of 46 cm (18 in).

- **1962** A massive avalanche and mudslide in Peru kills about 4,000 people.

- **1963** Hurricane Flora kills more than 7,000 in Haiti and Cuba.

- **1979** More than 100 mm (4 in) of rain causes flooding in South Wales. Cardiff is particularly badly affected when the River Taff in spate meets a high tide from the Bristol Channel.

- **1980** A heatwave in America starts forest fires, destroys crops, and dries up reservoirs. More than 1,000 people die.

- **1982** September monsoon floods in Orissa, India, kill at least 1,000 and leave five million homeless.

- **1984** A summer hailstorm lasting just 20 minutes bombards Munich, Germany, with giant hailstones and causes damage amounting to $1 billion.

A giant hailstone

The result of mudslides in Venezuela

- **1970** More than 400,000 die when a tropical cyclone produces a storm surge that floods the Ganges Delta.

- **1971** Hurricane Ginger wanders the North Atlantic, the Bermuda Triangle, and the coasts of North Carolina and Virginia, USA, for a record 31 days (20 of them with hurricane-force winds).

- **1974** On Christmas Day, Cyclone Tracy strikes Darwin, Australia, killing 50 people.

- **1974** Hurricane Fifi kills as many as 10,000 people in Honduras, destroys 80 per cent of the banana crop and drowns two-fifths of the country's cattle.

- **1977** In November, a tropical cyclone and storm surge strike Andhra Pradesh, India, killing 20,000 and making more than two million homeless. A few days later another cyclone kills more than 1,500 in Sri Lanka and southern India.

- **1985** Hurricane Elena's erratic path across the Gulf of Mexico results in the evacuation of nearly one million people. Elena finally makes landfall in Mississippi, USA, causing damages of $1.3 billion.

- **1988** Monsoon rains flood three-quarters of Bangladesh, killing more than 2,000 and making 30 million people homeless.

- **1992** Hurricane Andrew strikes the Bahamas, Florida and Louisiana, USA, killing 65 people and destroying 25,000 homes. It causes an estimated $20 billion damage.

- **1993** A three-day March blizzard kills more than 200 people in the USA.

- **1996** A tornado takes only half an hour to destroy 80 villages in Bangladesh, killing more than 440 people and injuring more than 32,000.

- **1997** Lightning kills 19 people in Andhra Pradesh, India, on 11 September.

- **1988** Monsoon rains flood three-quarters of Bangladesh, killing more than 2,000 and making 30 million people homeless.

- **1998** In early May, a black tide of mud sweeps through Sarno, Italy, killing more than 130 people and leaving 2,000 homeless.

- **1998** At least 2,500 people perish in an Indian heatwave in May and June.

- **1998** The Yangtze River, China, floods, killing more than 3,500 people, but affecting at least 230 million.

- **1998** At least 2,500 people die in July when a tsunami strikes Papua New Guinea.

- **1998** In September and October, floods along the River Nile in Sudan leave at least 200,000 people homeless.

- **1998** More than 11,000 die and 1.5 million are made homeless when Hurricane Mitch strikes Central America in October.

- **1999** Floods and mudslides in December kill at least 10,000 in Venezuela.

- **2000** Torrential rains in February cause the worst floods for 50 years in Mozambique. On 22 February Cyclone Eline hits Mozambique making the situation even worse.

- **2003** At least 200 people die, and more than 130,000 families are left homeless when heavy rains in May cause Sri Lanka's worst floods since 1947.

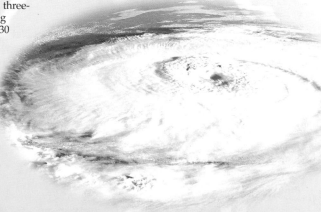

Hurricane Elena

Find out more

THERE ARE MANY WAYS of finding out more about the weather, and about extreme conditions around the world. Start by making or buying your own simple weather instruments, so that you can take your own measurements. You can keep a log of hurricanes and tornadoes, and follow the activities of the people who chase after them. You could investigate projects that are helping people in areas prone to drought or flooding, or go on a visit to a wind farm to see how people harness the weather's energy.

VISIT A WIND FARM
Wind farms use the power of wind to generate electricity. Visit a wind farm near you and discover some of the advantages of this renewable energy resource. Find out where it is best to position the farms, and how long you can expect wind turbines to last.

The generator converts the movement of the shaft into electricity

The blade turns to face the wind

USEFUL WEBSITES

- To find out about the Meteorological Office, see: **www.meto.govt.uk**
- For information on how to set up a weather station, go to: **www.meto.govt.uk/education/observations/index.html**
- For weather forecasts anywhere in the world and information about severe weather, go to: **http://weather.yahoo.com**
- To find out about people who follow hurricanes, see: **www.hurricanehunters.com**
- To find out about Australian storm chasing news, go to: **www.australiasevereweather.com/tornado.htm**
- For information about tornadoes, see: **www.stormtrack.org** and **www.nhc.noaa.gov/**

MONITOR THE WEATHER
Build or buy your own weather centre. Keep a daily log of weather measurements, such as temperature (daily maximum and minimum), air pressure, rainfall, and wind speed. If possible, you or your school could join MetLink International, an online project run by the Royal Meteorological Society. By doing so you will find out a great deal not only about your own weather but also about weather in other parts of the world as you compare your readings with those from groups in other countries.

HURRICANE CHASERS
Find out how teams in the USA and Australia track hurricanes in trucks and planes in order to learn more about them. They take photographs and measurements as they go. The aeroplanes attempt to fly right into the eye of the hurricane. Follow the latest news on the hurricane hunters website and the Australian severe weather website.

STOP THE DESERT

Many parts of the world suffer from a severe shortage of rain. Find out how people, animals, and plants manage to survive with so little water. In northern Africa, the drought, combined with overgrazing, and the removal of trees for firewood, is resulting in the expansion of the Sahara desert. Find out about the grass-planting projects that are trying to stop the spread of the desert.

GOOD FLOODING

Floods can cause huge amounts of damage, but there are cases where flooding can be beneficial. Sometimes it increases the fertility of the soil, while in other places it creates an important environment for wildlife. The Ouse Washes in Cambridgeshire flood every winter and as a result attract thousands of migrating birds.

About 7,000 migrating swans gather on the Ouse Washes each winter

Places to visit

THE CENTRE FOR ALTERNATIVE TECHNOLOGY, MACHYNLLETH, WALES

Visitors enter the centre via a water-balanced cliff railway. There are a wide range of interactive displays on wind, water, and solar power, as well as on energy efficiency, green transport and growing food organically. During the school holidays there are additional free activities for children. You can find out more about wind farms by looking at the wind turbine demonstration on **www.cat.org.uk/**.

THE NATIONAL SPACE CENTRE, EXPLORATION DRIVE, LEICESTER, ENGLAND

There is information on how we use satellites to keep an eye on the weather, and an interactive weather forecasting studio enables visitors to have a go at forecasting the weather.

THE THAMES RIVER BARRIER, LONDON, ENGLAND

Officially opened in May 1984, the Thames River Barrier provides flood control for the River Thames, including London. There are nine concrete piers, with ten openings, six of them for shipping. Steel gates can be raised from the riverbed if there is the threat of a high surge tide. Boat trips to the Thames Barrier depart from the centre of London and from Greenwich. It is worth visiting when the barrier gates are being tested.

THE WILDFOWL AND WETLANDS TRUST (WWT) OUSE WASHES RESERVE, WELNEY, CAMBRIDGESHIRE, ENGLAND

In the winter, thousands of migrating ducks and swans spend time here, while in the summer, redshanks, lapwings, and snipe breed on the reserve. For more information, go to: **www.wwt.org.uk/visit/welney/default.asp**

FLOOD WARNINGS

Contact the environment agency and find out more about flood alerts. Look at the floodline information page on **www.environment-agency.gov.uk**. Map your part of the country, marking areas that are prone to flooding, and investigate the reasons why flooding is common there. See if you can visit flood defences, such as the dykes in Norfolk, the Thames River Barrier, or these flood gates in Zeeland, Holland.

Glossary

ANEMOMETER An instrument for recording the speed and direction of winds.

ATMOSPHERE The gases surrounding the Earth and some other planets.

ATMOSPHERIC PRESSURE The push of the atmosphere on the Earth's surface.

AURORA Bands of light across the sky, visible near the North and South Poles.

AVALANCHE A fall of snow and ice down a mountain.

BARGRAPH A chart with vertical or horizontal bars showing amounts or quantities.

BAROCYCLONOMETER An early device used to calculate the position of an approaching cyclone. It measured atmospheric pressure and wind direction.

BAROMETER An instrument for measuring atmospheric pressure, to determine weather changes or altitude.

BEAUFORT SCALE An international scale of wind speed ranging from 0 (calm) to 12 (hurricane force).

BLIZZARD A strong, bitterly cold wind accompanied by heavy snow.

CLIMATE The usual, long-term weather conditions of an area.

CUMULONIMBUS CLOUD A billowing, white or dark-grey cloud that is very tall from top to bottom. Also known as a thunderhead, this type of cloud is associated with thunderstorms. The top of the cloud is often the shape of an anvil, and the bottom can be quite dark if it is full of rain or hail.

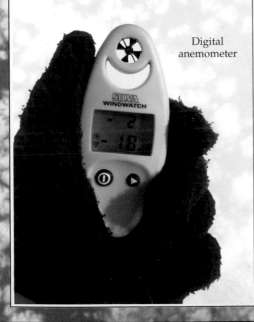
Digital anemometer

An early barometer

CYCLONE A violent tropical storm.

DEPRESSION A body of moving air that is below normal atmospheric pressure. Depressions often bring rain.

DOLDRUMS Areas near the equator where there are very light winds or calms.

DROUGHT A long period with very little rainfall.

DUST DEVIL A strong, miniature whirlwind that whips up dust and litter into the air.

EL NINO A warming of the eastern tropical Pacific Ocean. It occurs every few years and severely disrupts the weather pattern in the area.

FLASH FLOOD A sudden torrent, usually caused by a heavy storm.

FLOOD When a river or other area of water overflows and covers land that is normally dry.

FLOOD DEFENCES Dykes and other barriers constructed to protect land that is at risk from flooding.

FOG A mass of water droplets hanging in the air and reducing visibility.

FORK LIGHTNING A zig-zag form of lightning.

GALE A strong wind of force 8 on the Beaufort Scale, or between 62 and 74 kph (39 and 46 mph).

GLOBAL WARMING An increase in the average temperature worldwide, believed to be caused by the greenhouse effect.

GREENHOUSE EFFECT The warming up of the Earth, as increases in carbon dioxide trap more of the infrared radiation emitted by the Earth's surface.

HAILSHAFT The column of hail falling from a hail-bearing cloud.

HAILSTONE A pellet of ice falling from cumulonimbus clouds that have very strong rising air currents.

HAILSTORM A storm during which hail falls.

HUMIDITY A measure of the amount of moisture in the air.

HURRICANE A severe storm that is often very destructive, also called a tropical cyclone. The storms are known as typhoons in the Pacific Ocean, and cyclones in the Indian Ocean.

HURRICANE CHASERS People who chase after hurricanes in order to find out more about them.

A meteorologist examines a rainfall monitor

HYGROMETER An instrument that measures the amount of moisture in the air.

ICE AGE A period of time when ice covers a large part of the Earth's land surface.

ICE STORM Extreme weather in which water in the air freezes and coats everything in ice.

JET STREAM A long current of air about 12 km (7.4 miles) above the Earth's surface. The jet streams are hundreds of kilometres long, 100 km (60 miles) wide, and about a kilometre (0.6 miles) deep. They can reach speeds of 300–500 kph (200–300 mph).

LANDSLIDE The slipping of a large amount of rock and soil down the side of a mountain or cliff.

LIGHTNING A bright flash of light that occurs during a thunderstorm when electricity is discharged either between two clouds or between a cloud and the Earth.

LIGHTNING CONDUCTOR A metal strip fixed between the highest part of a building and the ground to provide a safe route to Earth for the lightning.

METEOROLOGY The study of the Earth's atmosphere, of the ways in which weather forms, and of methods of forecasting the weather.

Under the Wave off Kanagawa by Hokusai

MONSOON A seasonal wind in South Asia. In summer it blows from the southwest and brings heavy rains; in winter it blows from the northeast.

PRECIPITATION Moisture falling to Earth in the form of rain, snow, hail, sleet, or dew, when water vapour condenses in the atmosphere.

RAINBOW An arc of colours across the sky caused by the refraction and reflection of the sun's rays through the rain.

SANDSTORM A strong wind that whips up clouds of sand, especially in a desert.

SMOG A mixture of smoke and fog.

SNOWSTORM A storm with heavy snow.

SPATE The fast flow, or sudden rush of water in a river.

STORM SURGE A dramatic high tide that may produce flooding. Caused by the sudden pressure drop and high winds of an offshore storm.

SUPERCELL A particularly large pocket of rising air that brings massive amounts of water into a thundercloud. Supercells can generate tornadoes and waterspouts.

TEMPERATURE A measurement of how hot a body or substance is.

THERMOMETER An instrument used to measure temperature, usually with a thin column of liquid that expands or contracts within a sealed tube.

THERMOSCOPE A device that indicates variations in temperature without measuring their amounts.

THUNDERBOLT A flash of lightning accompanied by thunder.

THUNDERCLAP A loud cracking noise caused by atmospheric gases expanding rapidly when heated suddenly by lightning.

THUNDERHEAD A towering cumulonimbus cloud that is electrically charged. A thunderhead is dark in colour because it is full of rain or hail.

THUNDERSTORM A storm caused by strong rising air currents, featuring thunder, lightning, and usually heavy rain or hail.

TIDAL WAVE An unusually large wave not actually caused by the tides at all, but by an earthquake. Properly called a tsunami.

TORNADO Also known as a cyclone, a whirlwind or a twister. A violent storm in which winds whirl around a small area of very low pressure. There is usually a dark, funnel-shaped cloud reaching down to Earth and causing immense damage.

TORNADO ALLEY The name given to the parts of Kansas, Missouri and Oklahoma, USA, that are most at risk from tornadoes.

A satellite

TRADE WINDS Winds blowing towards the equator, from approximately 30° N and 30° S. They blow from the northeast in the northern hemisphere and from the southeast in the southern hemisphere.

TSUNAMI A huge, destructive wave that is often caused by an earthquake on the seabed.

VORTEX A whirling mass of liquid or gas. The vortex of a tornado or hurricane is at its centre.

WATERSPOUT A whirling water column drawn up from the surface by a whirlwind travelling over water.

WEATHER SATELLITE Devices that orbit the Earth and send back data to help scientists forecast the weather.

WHIRLWIND A column of air whirling around an area of low pressure, and moving across the land or the surface of the ocean.

Flooding caused by monsoon rains in Vietnam

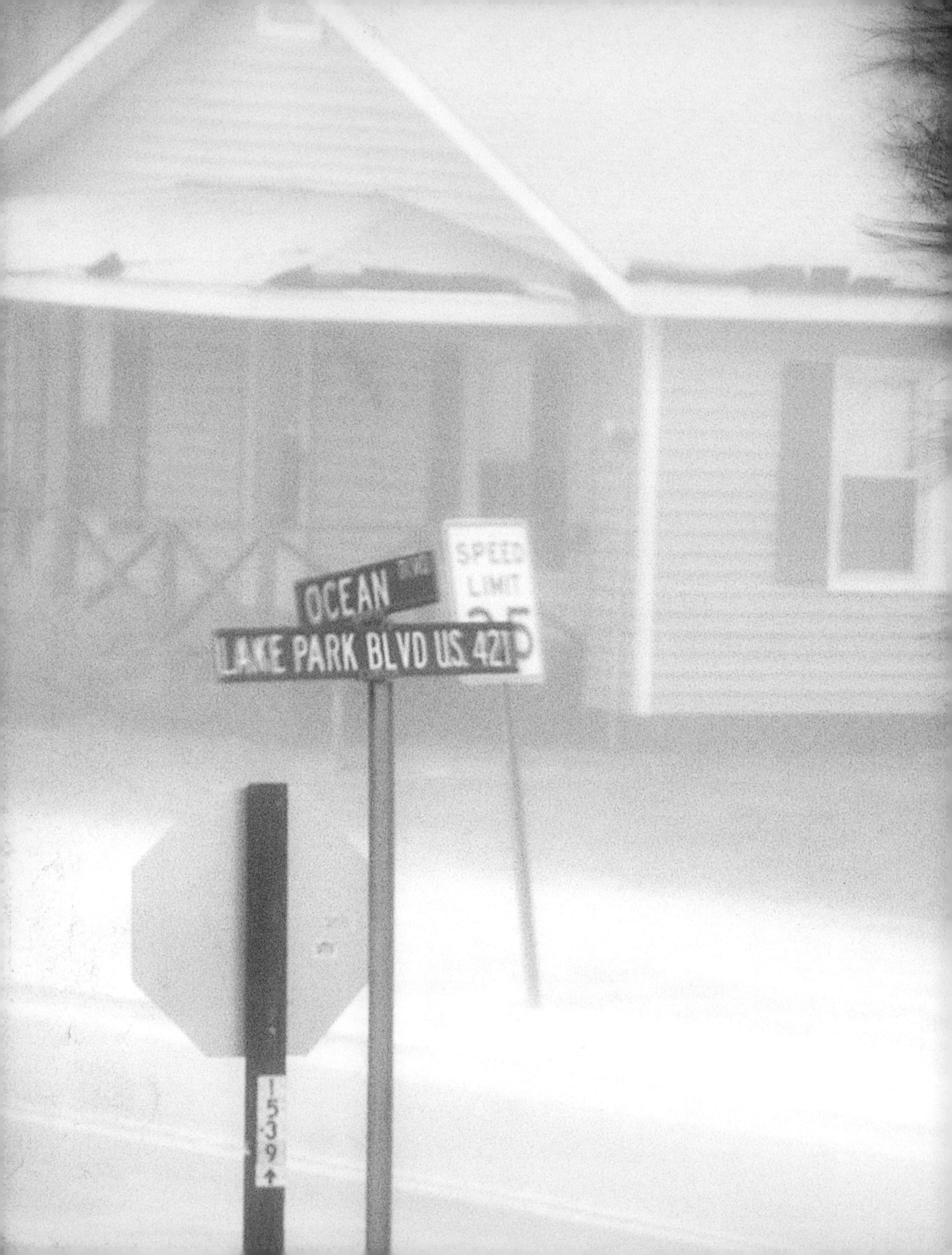
OCEAN
LAKE PARK BLVD U.S. 421
SPEED
LIMIT
1539

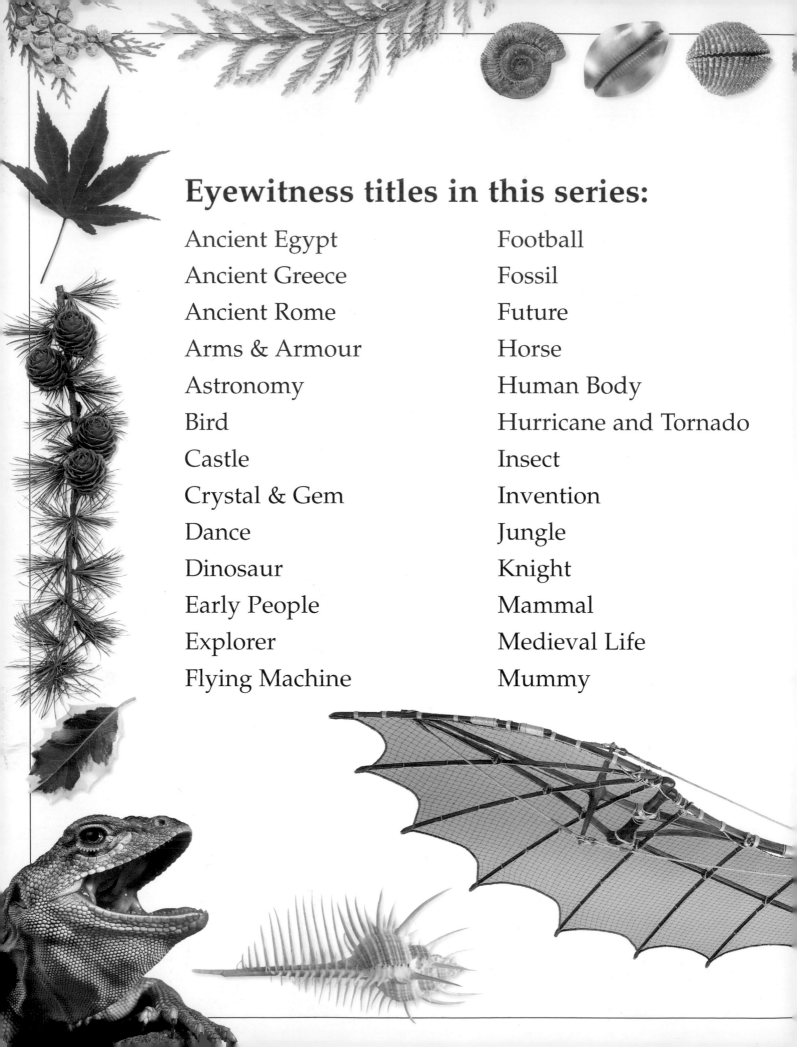

Eyewitness titles in this series:

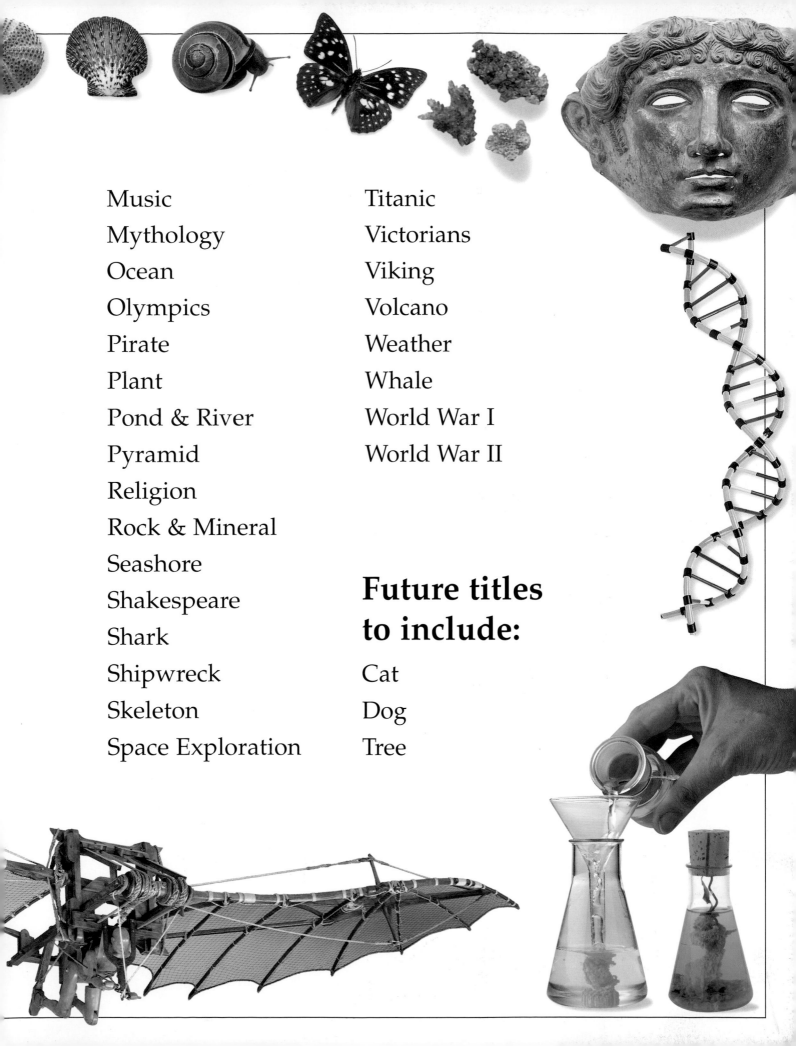

Future titles to include:

Index

Acknowledgements

Dorling Kindersley would like to thank:
Sheila Collins for design assistance.

Indexer: Chris Bernstein

Illustrators: Eric Thomas and John Woodcock

Photographers: Peter Anderson, Jeoff Brightling, Jane Burton, Peter Chadwick, Andy Crawford, Geoff Dann, Mike Dunning, Steve Gorton, Frank Greenaway, Ellen Howden, Colin Keates, Dave King, Andrew Nelmerm, Janet Peckham, Kim Sayer, Karl Shone, Andreas Von Einsiedel, Jerry Young, and Michel Zabé

Picture credits
The publisher would like to thank the following for their kind permission to reproduce their photographs:

t=top, b=below, l=left, r=right, c=centre:

Alison Anholt White: 16c.
Ardea London Ltd: Francois Gohier 12bl; M. Watson 39bl.
Associated Press Ap: 37tl, 41tl, 41bl; SLF Jennings 30-31; Topham 48tr.
Bridgeman Art Library, London / New York: Thor's fight with the Giants, 1872 by Winge, Marten Eskil 1825-96, Nationalmuseum, Stockholm, Sweden; Plato and Aristotle, detail of the School of Athens, 1510-1511 (fresco), Vatican Museum and Galleries 8bc.
British Museum, London: 9ca, 9cr.
Bruce Coleman Ltd: Jules Cowan; 53tr Jeff Foott 4b, 16-17; Johnny Johnson 51bc; Allan G. Potts 54-55b.
Corbis UK Ltd: 39tl, 39r; Bettmann 10cr, 24crb, 40cl, 43c; Lowell Georgia 6tr, 38tl; David Muench 52cl; Galen Rowell 39cr; Dave Bartruff 64l; Bettmann 62br; Rick Doyle 61bl; El Universal/ Sygma 63cl; Chris Golley 60tr; Historical Picture Archive 67l;

Aaron Horowitz 60bl; George McCarthy 65cl; Sygma 64br; A & J Verkaik 62-63 bckgrd; Patrick Ward 65br; Steve Wilkings 60-61 bckgrd; Michael S. Yamashita 67b.
Sylvia Cordaiy Photo Library Ltd: Nigel Rolstone 24-25b.
Ecoscene: Nick Hawkes 38bl.
Environmental Images: John Arnold 45cr.
E.T. Archive: Guildhall Library 52cr.
European Space Agency: 67tr;
Mary Evans Picture Library: 24bc, 28cl, 62cl.
Glasgow Museums, The Burrell Collection: 42tl.
Ronald Grant Archive: WB & Universal 22-23cl.
Robert Harding Picture Library: 13cl, 13b, 34-35a; Jon Gardley 45tr; Dr. A.C. Waltham 34-35b; 68-69 bckgrd.
Hulton Getty: Fox 34cr; Tony Waltham 41tr; G. Williams Photos 36tr; Keystone 32cl; Painted by Stephen Pearce, engraved by John Scott 16tl.
Hutchison Library: 33r.
ICRC: Clive Shirley 49bl.
INAH: Mexican Museum Authority, Michael Zabe 9bl.
Kristen Klaver: 47clb, 47bl.
FLPA – Images of nature: 30-31ca; J.C. Allen 26bl; D. Hoadley 22-23cr; H. Hoflinger 20cr; NRC 27cl; R. Jennings 56c; S. Jonasson 15br.
Magnum: Bruce Davidson 17ca; Steve McCurry 40bl.
Gene Moore: 26-27, 27tl, 27cr.
N.A.S.A.: 4tr, 4c, 6cl, 4cl, 28-29, 47br, 58tr, 58-59c, 58b, 59c, 59bl, 59br, 59t; 6bc, 18cl.
National Maritime Museum, London: 10cr.
Nature Picture Library: Mike Lane 65cl;
Courtesy of the National Science Foundation: 45tl, 45cla.
NHPA: A.N.T. 21cr.
NOAA: Dennis J. Sigrist, International Tsunami Information Centre, Honolulu, Hawaii 34bl.
Novosti: A. Varfolomeyer 26tr.
Oxford Scientific Films: Daniel J.

Cox 44cl; Warren Faidley 6bl, 19br, 25a, 28tl; Michael Fogden 42c; Richard Henman 54bl; Mantis Wildlife Films 51cr; Colin Monteath, Hegehog House 32b; Ian West 22-23clb; Stan Osolinksi 56cl; Stouffer Enterprises Inc./ Animals Animals 14b.
Panos Pictures: Trygue Bolstad 43tl; Heidi Bradner 13tr; Jerry Callow 8cl; Neil Cooper 43cb; Jeremy Hartley 42tr, 58cl; Sim Holmes 4tc, 28bl; Zed Nelson 28tr; Clive Shirley 54c, 55bc; © Tatlow 55tr.
PA News Photo Library: EPA/Pool 16tr.
Pitt Rivers Museum, Oxford: 9cra.
Planet Earth Pictures: Georgette Douwma 55tl; Jiri Lochman 55cr.
John E. Purchase: 56bl.
Rex Features: 16cl, 31tr, 40br, 41cl, 48bl; Jean Yves Desfoux 36cl; Sipa Press 20-21.
Courtesy Of The Rosenberg Library, Galveston, Texas: 30bl.
Royal British Columbia Museum: 52bl.
Scala: Museo della Scienza Firenze 4tl, 6br, 10br, 10l, 11bl; S. Maria Novella (farmacia), Firenze 11c.
Science Photo Library: Eric Bernard, Jerrican 36bl; Jean-Loup Charmet 24c; Jim Goodwin 48cl; Ben Johnson 34cl; Damien Lovegrove 56crb; Pete Menzel 24cl NASA. 25bc; NASA GSFC 54tr; Claude Nuridsany & Marie Perennesu 5tl, 36cr; David Parker 46bl, 47tr, 53cl; Pekka Parviainen 57clb; Fred K. Smith 5bc, 18tr; 66-67 bckgrd; Brian Brake 62tr; Cape Grim B.A.P.S / Simon Fraser 66r; Simon Fraser 66bl; NASA 63br; NCAR 63t; Kazuyoshi Nomachi 65tl; Claude Nuridsany & Marie Perennou 61cr; Pekka Parviainen 60tl, 61tl; Victor de Schwanberg 64-65 bckgrd.
Still Pictures: Adrian Arbib 49br; Nigel Dickenson 48br; Filho-UNEP 55c; G. Grifiths/ Christian Aid 54clb; Olivier Langrand 50cb; Andre Maslennikor 42bc; Gil Moti 32cr;

Hartmut Schwarzbach 42br, 49tr; Hjalte Tin 49cl; UNEP. 57.
Courtesy of Jeff Piotrowski/ Storm Productions Inc. USA: 6cr, 20cl, 20clb, 20bl, 22-23tr, 22-23br.
Tony Stone Images: 52-53b; Vince Streano 31crb.
Stock Shot: Gary Pearl 38cb; Peter Quenault 38tr; Jess Stock 13tl, 38cl.
Sygma: 31cra, 31br; Paul/Pierre Pollin 37b; Claude Poulet 44tr.
Topham Picturepoint: 22-23r.
Travel Ink: David Toase 34tr.
Weatherstock: Warren Faidley 6tl, 7tr, 12tr, 13cr, 37tr, 46bc, 47tl, 57cl, 59r.